RVUs at Work

RELATIVE VALUE UNITS IN THE MEDICAL PRACTICE

— SECOND EDITION —

By **Max Reiboldt**, CPA
Justin Chamblee, MAcc, CPA
Coker Group

GREENBRANCH
PUBLISHING

PO Box 208
Phoenix, MD 21131
Phone: (800) 933-3711
Fax: (410) 329-1510
Email: info@greenbranch.com
Websites: www.greenbranch.com, www.mpmnetwork.com, www.soundpractice.net, www.codapedia.com

No patent liability is assumed with respect to the use of the information contained herein. Although every precaution has been taken in the preparation of this book, the publisher and the authors assume no responsibility for errors or omissions. Nor is any liability assumed from damages resulting from the use of the information contained herein. For information, Greenbranch Publishing, PO Box 208, Phoenix, MD 21131.

The strategies contained herein may not be suitable for every situation. This publication is designed to provide general medical practice management information and is sold with the understanding that neither the author nor the publisher is engaged in rendering legal, accounting, ethical, or clinical advice. If legal or other expert advice is required, the services of a competent professional person should be sought.

Greenbranch Publishing books are available at special quantity discounts for bulk purchases as premiums, fund-raising, or educational use. info@greenbranch.com or (800) 933-3711.

14   8 7 6 5 4 3 2 1

Copyedited, typeset, indexed, and printed in the United States of America

CPT™® is a registered trademark of the American Medical Association

PUBLISHER
Nancy Collins

EDITORIAL ASSISTANT
Jennifer Weiss

BOOK DESIGNER
Laura Carter
Carter Publishing Studio

INDEX
Robert A. Saigh

COPYEDITOR
Patricia George

ABOUT THE AUTHORS

Max Reiboldt, CPA, President/CEO

 Max Reiboldt is president and CEO of Coker Group with over 40 years of total experience, the last 21 years specifically focused on healthcare. Mr. Reiboldt provides sound tactical and strategic solutions to hospitals, medical practices, health systems, and other healthcare entities through keen analysis and problem solving. Working with organizations of all sizes, Reiboldt engages in consulting projects with organizations nationwide. His expertise encompasses physician/hospital alignment initiatives, hospital service line development, clinical integration initiatives, financial analyses, mergers and acquisitions, hospital and practice strategic planning, ancillary services development, PHO/IPA/MSO development, practice appraisals, and most recently, "accountable care era" consultation. As the industry moves to adapting to many changes in response to healthcare reform, Reiboldt is providing hands-on consultation to hospitals, health systems, and large practices.

Reiboldt has led the Firm's growth since 1996 to its position today as one of the leading healthcare consulting firms in the U.S. and abroad. He is an accomplished public speaker on healthcare management topics and has authored or contributed to many of Coker Group's 60-plus books. Recent titles include *The Healthcare Executive's Guide to ACO Strategies* (©2012 Health Leaders Media), and the recently published *The Healthcare Executive's Guide to Physician-Hospital Alignment* (©2013, Health Leaders Media).

A graduate of Harding University, Reiboldt is a licensed certified public accountant in Georgia and Louisiana, and a member of the American Institute of Certified Public Accountants, Healthcare Financial Management Association, and American Society of Appraisers. Mr. Reiboldt is also a member of the American College of Healthcare Executives. Contact Max at mreiboldt@cokergroup.com.

Justin Chamblee, MAcc, CPA, Vice President

Justin Chamblee works with clients in a variety of strategic and financial areas, mainly dealing with physician compensation and hospital-physician transactions. This includes the development and redesign of physician compensation plans for private practices and hospital-employed settings, as well as providing guidance to hospitals, physicians, and legal counsel as to the appropriateness of transactions between a hospital and a physician.

Justin frequently speaks on conference faculties in the healthcare industry and has authored several books in cooperation with publishers such as Greenbranch Publishing, American Medical Association, and HealthLeaders Media. Prior to joining Coker Group, he worked as a senior associate for PricewaterhouseCoopers in their audit practice.

Justin has a BBA in Accounting and a Master's of Accounting from Abilene Christian University. He is licensed as a Certified Public Accountant in the State of Texas and is a member of the American Institute of Certified Public Accountants. Contact Justin at jchamblee@cokergroup.com.

CONTRIBUTORS

Frank Allen

Frank Allen is a senior associate with Coker Group and has more than 20 years of experience in financial services. Mr. Allen has specialized experience in hospital/physician alignment, healthcare valuations, compensation reviews, financial modeling, fairness/FMV opinions, and financial analyses specifically for Coker's financial advisory services and alignment teams. Mr. Allen has extensive experience in process improvement, financial reporting, and budgeting with prior experience that includes P&L responsibility for national and international companies with multi-site divisions and gross revenues of more than $250 million and budget tracking responsibility up to $1.2 billion. He holds a BBA in accounting from Harding University.

Thomas D. Anthony, JD, Esq.

Tom Anthony, chair of the Frost Brown Todd's Healthcare Industry practice, advises his clients on Stark, Anti-Kickback, and all other healthcare regulatory matters. In addition, he serves as counsel to hospitals regarding clinically integrated networks, medical staff bylaws, physician relations, acquisition of medical groups, corporate governance, acquisitions of outpatient and ancillary facilities, strategic alliances and joint ventures, the establishment of provider-based facilities, executive employment agreements, Medicare compliance, contracting, and employment matters. Mr. Anthony also represents several long-term care chains in mergers/acquisitions, regulatory, patient rights, and financings. Holding a BS from Miami University, Mr. Anthony received his JD from Case Western Reserve University School of Law.

Jeannie Cagle, RN, BSN, CPC

Jeannie Cagle serves as a practice management consultant for Coker Group. Her projects include working with physician groups in completing coding analyses, medical chart audits, and practice assessments. Engagements by hospitals and practices encompass coordination of compliance audits and corporate integrity agreements, including serving as an internal review officer. Analyzing EMR software from a coding perspective and conducting return-on-investment analyses for implementation of EMR software in medical practices are also projects that Ms. Cagle completes. An experienced public speaker who incorporates a practical and keen approach to tedious subjects, she places a current emphasis on physician education and training in coding and compliance issues. Ms. Cagle holds a BSN from Harding University.

Aimee Greeter, MPH

Aimee Greeter is a senior manager at Coker Group with specialized experience in alignment, strategic planning, accountable care responsiveness, compensation, mergers and collaborations, operational issues, and financial management. Ms. Greeter focuses on working with nonprofit and for-profit hospitals and health systems of all sizes, and larger single and multi-specialty physician practices. A popular program speaker, she is frequently engaged by highly respected organizations across the nation. Her accomplishments include the authorship of numerous articles and books. Ms. Greeter attained a BS with honors in human biology from Michigan State University and an MPH in health policy and management from the Rollins School of Public Health at Emory University.

Deborah Hill, MBA, CMPE, CPC, CPC-I, CHC

Deborah Hill, manager of practice management services, is responsible for managing for Coker Group the delivery of services to large physician practices, hospitals, and healthcare systems. She provides counsel in the areas of operational and revenue cycle assessments and provides interim oversight in these areas, supervising the process for all provider enrollment and credentialing on managed care plans, reviewing and negotiating managed care contracts, supervising the coding and audit process, and initiating training and recommendations to providers and staff for appropriate documentation, billing, compliance plan design, and implementation. Ms. Hill attained a BBA in management from the University of West Georgia and an MBA in business administration with a focus in healthcare from Brenau University.

David Julian, CPA

David Julian, CPA, is a manager with Coker Group who has more than 20 years of experience in financial services. Mr. Julian has extensive experience in planning and implementing accounting policies and procedures. His robust background in accounting, financial analysis, and problem solving gives him insight into clients' unique financial needs and goals. His myriad operational experience provides leadership in the development and evaluation of short- and long-term strategic financial objectives. Mr. Julian holds a BS in accounting from Lipscomb University.

Madiha Khan, MPH

Madiha Khan, staff associate for Coker Group's financial advisory and alignment services (FAAS), works with the FAAS team on strategic planning, accountable care responsiveness, and compensation projects. Her experience also includes presentation development for Coker's various speaking engagements and Webinars, and the co-authorship of a variety of healthcare articles and publications. Ms. Khan is a graduate of the University of Virginia with a BA in psychology and minor in biology. She received an MPH in health policy and management from the Rollins School of Public Health at Emory University.

Rick Langosch, FHFMA

Rick Langosch, senior vice president, is a seasoned healthcare executive at Coker Group, with over 25 years of experience managing operations and finance in hospitals and physician practices. At Coker, Mr. Langosch uses that experience to assist clients with operational assessments (both hospital and physician practices), revenue cycle challenges (including managed care negotiating and credentialing assistance) and strategic planning. He also is involved in service line analyses and productivity analyses, providing leadership and hands-on participation during interim and long-term management engagements. A graduate of Eastern Illinois University with a BS in business-accountancy, Mr. Langosch is also a Fellow of the Healthcare Financial Management Association.

Mark Reiboldt BA, MSc

Mark Reiboldt, vice president of Coker Group, provides counsel on strategy and financial consulting engagements for healthcare organizations across the nation. His experience as a financial analyst in the financial services and communication sectors has included engagements involving multi-billion dollar transactions. Mr. Reiboldt serves on the boards of numerous for-profit and not-for-profit organizations within healthcare and other arenas. Mr. Reiboldt received a BA in political science from Georgia State University and an MSc in financial economics from the University of London.

Steven Twaddle, FACMPE

Steve Twaddle has worked as an executive healthcare administrator for 20 years with a number of hospital and physician-owned organizations. With a vast amount of experience relating to multi-specialty and integrated delivery systems, Mr. Twaddle specializes in strategic planning, group governance, and daily operational practice management services. His background has allowed him to work with hospital and physician leadership to facilitate the best decisions concerning operations, growth, profitability, and regulatory compliance. Mr. Twaddle has written numerous articles on such topics as practice management, compensation, integration, trust, and culture of organizations. He is currently the managing principal of Grinnell & Twaddle Associates, a healthcare consulting company specializing in leadership and organizational development. It is there he created the Healthcare Trust Matrix (TM) assessment tool to identify specific interpersonal and intra-organizational trust issues between hospital and employed/community physicians. Mr. Twaddle holds an MBA and an M Mgt in health services management from the University of Dallas.

John Vandermosten, CFA

John Vandermosten, CFA, manager at Coker Group, works with clients in a variety of strategic and financial areas, including health practice valuations, physician compensation, and hospital/physician transactions. Mr. Vandermosten has an MBA from Texas A&M University, an MA from Tulane University, and a BA from San Diego State University. He has also earned the Chartered Financial Analyst designation and is a member of the CFA Society of Dallas.

Yong Zhang, CPA

Yong Zhang, CPA, is a manager in Coker's financial advisory and alignment services service line. She works with healthcare organizations of all sizes and in many different sectors within the healthcare industry. Empowered by her strong financial foundation in the areas of business valuation, US GAAP, financial investing, and federal taxation, Ms. Zhang provides services in a variety of areas, including valuations and appraisals, mergers/acquisitions/divestitures, pro forma financial statement compilations and analyses, and other areas of financial and operational analyses. Ms. Zhang has successfully completed all comprehensive examinations for and is currently working through the accreditation process to become an accredited senior appraiser in business valuation from the American Society of Appraisers. Ms. Zhang holds a BA in accounting from Fudan University and earned her master of accountancy from the University of Georgia.

ACKNOWLEDGMENTS

Change occurs rapidly in health care, as evidenced by the need for a second edition of *RVUs at Work: Relative Value Units in the Medical Practice* within three years of its publication in 2010. The updates and new chapters in the Second Edition address the pertinent adjustments in how RVUs affect the spectrum of care delivery and the subsequent payment for the work involved. The intent of this edition is to update readers so they can respond to current trends in RVU utilization and to consider how RVUs will be used in the era of accountable care.

As editor, I would like to acknowledge the expertise of many contributors who specialize in the areas described by the chapter titles. In addition to the Coker Group team, a special note of appreciation goes to Thomas Anthony, Esq., for his expertise in health care law. Steven Twaddle's extensive knowledge of increasing productivity via RVUs is also a valuable addition to this project.

It is always a pleasure to work with Greenbranch Publishing, and I appreciate the confidence that Nancy Collins extends to the Coker Group team of contributors. Nancy and Jennifer Weiss are a dream team to work with.

Kay B. Stanley, FACMPE, Editor

CONTENTS

History and Background of RVUs

Since the 1950s, systems for establishing relative values to services have been a part of the medical world. Undoubtedly, they have evolved since then and now take the shape of relative value units (RVUs). Even with the advent of health reform and an era based on accountability, cost of care, and quality, RVUs have continued to play an integral role among healthcare entities. With provider compensation, payer reimbursement, and productivity always being at the forefront of healthcare, a thorough understanding of RVUs is imperative.

An understanding of RVUs and how they fit into the medical practice first requires an overview of the various meanings and interpretations of productivity. Within medical practices, provider productivity can be measured in a number of ways:

- *Gross charges.* Typically this represents the "full fee schedule" of the practice. The practice sets the gross charge of each code at the highest appropriate level that payers will reimburse. Gross charges may be established at various standards or benchmarks. Some practices may establish their fee schedule (and therefore their gross charge total) at 200% of Medicare rates, while others may set their fee schedule at 150% of Medicare or varied percentages by code.

- *Net charges.* Although fee schedules are established at a reasonably high rate to ensure no single payer reimburses more than the full fee schedule rate, ultimately virtually all charges must be adjusted. These adjustments are mainly a result of contractual allowances but sometimes they may be attributable to a bad debt factor. All gross charges are adjusted downward to derive net or adjusted charges, which can vary significantly among practices, based on their approach to establishing a fee schedule and a gross charge amount. In theory, however, net or adjusted charges are those amounts that should be collected.

- *Gross collections.* Gross collections are the dollars actually collected from the payers after billings are submitted and contractual allowances are considered. These collections are prior to the issuances of any refunds that may result from any overpayments or payments that are determined to be incorrect and later adjusted. While in theory they should closely mirror the net or adjusted charge figure, this does not always occur, especially when the contractual allowance amount is an estimate and is not adjusted until later to mirror the actual amounts collected.

- *Net receipts.* Net receipts are calculated after all refunds and adjustments have been applied to the original amount received. In theory, this amount should be close to the adjusted charge total but may not be exactly the same amount; hence, a periodic adjustment of the net or adjusted charges to the actual figure collected is needed.

Other forms of tracking productivity exist. They include patient encounters and number of procedures, both of which can be collected with relative accuracy. However, due to varying standards, using such metrics can often lead to difficulty in gleaning any significant or truly accurate productivity measurements. For example, an encounter for a pediatrician differs considerably from an encounter for a surgeon. A basic clinic encounter for a surgeon is not nearly as significant, and in fact as a postoperative encounter, may entail no additional revenue compared to the actual surgical procedure that was performed earlier. On the other hand, in general, every pediatric patient encounter should generate some form of billed charges.

Despite the array of productivity measures, very few establish a truly consistent standard of measurement within the context of performance. Gross charges may be used as a standard, because they are calculated prior to any adjustments for contractual allowances, bad debts, etc. However, gross charges can be changed easily at the press of a button with any adjustments to the fee schedule being up to the practice's decision. For example, if the practice increases its fee schedule, the total gross charges will increase but the actual amount of collections may not increase commensurately. Using gross charges to measure productivity can be misleading for both practice administrators and providers as it is unlikely that the true revenue realized has actually changed.

This is where RVUs come in to play, so to speak. Today, RVUs are the prevailing system for monitoring physician productivity and determining their allowable reimbursement.

Medicare annually establishes a physician fee schedule based on current procedural terminology (CPT) codes to determine payment for more than 7,500 physician services. The payment for each service depends on the RVUs, which rank on a common scale to the resources used to provide each service. As such, RVUs have attempted (quite successfully, in fact) to define the relative resources that go into the derivation of each individual code, which ultimately becomes each code's RVU value.

A total RVU value is comprised of three components: the expenses of the physician's practice, the professional liability (malpractice) insurance component, and the overall physician work or professional component. Although the actual percentages of each component differ across services, the approximate Medicare expenditures for the work, practice expense, and professional liability are 52%, 44%, and 4% of the total RVU value, respectively. The calculation used by Medicare to determine the value of the reimbursement entails multiplying a predetermined and assigned dollar conversion factor by each RVU.[1] This is the same regardless of the specialty of the physician, which also establishes greater

---

[1] In 2013, the conversion factor is $34.0230.

standardization. While it is adjusted for geographic differences in costs and other factors, RVUs still represent the greatest level of standardization for reimbursement and productivity.

Since their adoption, RVUs undeniably remains the most accurate methodology for interpreting operating results within the practice, and specifically, tracking and analyzing physician productivity.

A primary focus of this book will be a discussion of physician productivity in the context of RVUs and the changing healthcare landscape. To that end, we will make relevant applications of RVUs in medical practices for measuring physician productivity and overall job performance, factoring in considerations specific to the accountable care era. It is important to remember that despite the changes being rolled out by federal and state regulators, RVUs are still valuable measurements of performance relative to cost of delivery of physician services. The three components of RVUs are testament to this. Therefore, this book will consider RVUs using various frameworks, including physician productivity, practice overhead, and strategic planning for the accountable care era.

OUR RVU HISTORY

In the 1980s, the Centers for Medicare and Medicaid (CMS)[2] partially funded a Harvard School of Public Health-based study analyzing both resources and costs attributable to the delivery of physician services. The government's desire for a standardized system were primarily driven by rising Medicare costs, inequitable compensation for physician services and the noticeable influence of income on recent medical school graduates relative to their career paths. RVUs, as we know them, were adopted by the medical community over two decades ago as a result of this study after its analysis and conclusions resulted in the introduction of the resource-based relative value scale (RBRVS). The RBRVS system was introduced in 1992 and provided a format for describing, quantifying, and reimbursing the physician services of a single practice or similar practices relative to one another across all areas of medicine. The RBRVS system also applied the same three components of physician services' work, practice expense, and professional liability to its evaluation and management structure.

Moving it one step further, the RVU was then assigned, based on individual CPT codes. The CPT structure was developed by the American Medical Association as a standardized coding system. This coding system is currently used by Medicare, Medicaid, and virtually all private insurers that reimburse physician practices. During its initial adoption by Medicare, three individual conversion factors existed to transform RVUs into dollars, separated by type of service (e.g., primary care, specialty care, and surgical services). Six years later, one general conversion factor replaced this three-tiered arrangement. The 2013 conversion factor is $34.0230, but this value is evaluated and adjusted annually.

An RVU describes a unit of work (i.e., productivity) for each CPT code within that overall organized system of structure. For each CPT code, each of the three

---

[2] Known at that time as the Health Care Financing Administration (HCFA).

components is assigned an RVU and then summed to create the total RVU for that specific code. Medicare's reimbursement to providers is equal to the product of the conversion factor and the total RVU, which is the combination of the relative value units of their work-only component (i.e., wRVU), practice expenses, and professional liability insurance premiums. Because of these components, RVUs vary by service. For example, simple procedures have lower RVUs, and thus lower compensation rates, than more complex surgeries, which would be compensated at a higher rate due to greater RVU values, which are derived from a higher level of physician difficulty or greater associated practice expenses. This process is significant because it concerns all physicians, not just those who accept Medicare beneficiaries, as many commercial payers and Medicaid base their fee schedules on Medicare's rates. Thus, the value placed on each Medicare-sponsored physician service in terms of RVUs has an enormous impact on all national healthcare costs.

RVUs can easily become a resulting measurement of productivity in that they are "payer blind." For example, a 99213 evaluation and management (E&M) code carries the same RVU weight regardless of what the payer or patient actually pays. This lends consistency in both definition and accounting and performance evaluation relative to total RVU productivity. The methodology for assigning RVU values to medical services is a somewhat complex system, and until recently, also a bit controversial. When a new code is approved through the CPT process, it is actually subjected to the American Medical Association's Relative Value Scale Update Committee (RUC). The RUC was created in 1991 by the American Medical Association to act as an advisory group to CMS to estimate the relative amount of work that goes into physician services and make recommendations. The RUC has an advisory committee composed of one delegate from each of the 109 specialty societies in the American Medical Association. This committee is instrumental in the process of determining physician work values. Each advisory committee member attends RUC meetings and presents information on behalf of their specialty. After advisory committee presentations and long discussions, RUC members vote on the proposed values by secret electronic ballot. A two-thirds majority is required to send a relative value recommendation to CMS.

This process becomes even more complex when considering Medicare's budget neutrality requirement. In effect, this means that every additional dollar allocated to a given service will entail a dollar less for those members who do not use a given code. In this way, the RUC is responsible only for dividing up a given amount of Medicare dollars and not for deciding how much money is actually spent. The RUC must consider this in the process, which often results in some questions about (even potential disagreement with) RVU values.[3] Each year, CMS releases values for new and revised procedures, and every five years, CMS performs a comprehensive review of these values. Though CMS is officially responsible for making these adjustments, it typically accepts approximately 90% of the recommendations made by the RUC. As such, this process typically is handled

---

[3]Geographic Adjustment Factor: The three GPCI components can be combined in a composite GPCI or GAF by weighing each by the share of Medicare Payments accounted for by the work; practice expense and PLI components. CMS is required by statue to review the GPCI code valuations every three years and roll out any changes over the subsequent two years.

through the RUC; but even before that, interested parties may submit specific codes that they believe are inappropriately valued. These are then considered and weighed within the overall balance of any reassignment of values. Data are accumulated and used to form recommendations on how best to change a code's value. RUC ultimately reviews the data and submits its recommendations to CMS for appropriate action.

Despite having a procedure in place for re-evaluation, several critics of the RUC process have started to speak up, particularly in light of recent government changes. Specifically, primary care providers are growing increasingly concerned about the overwhelming majority of specialty physicians in the RUC body, outnumbering those who represent primary care services. Moreover, critics are taking issue with the seemingly automatic approval of RUC recommendations with little inquiry by CMS, and consequently, the considerable control the RUC has over the billions of Medicare dollars spent annually.

Other controversies surfaced relative to Medicare conversion factor, which is a significant part of the overall RVU, and even before that, RBRVS consideration. That factor is a dollar amount wherein each CPT code's total RVU value is multiplied to obtain the reimbursement paid by Medicare for the specific service under consideration. The conversion factor is updated annually by CMS and its calculation is based on an estimated sustainable growth rate (SGR), which is the target rate of growth in spending for physician services. The conversion factor, then, is an outcome of an analysis that is based on legislative requirements and the need to correlate actual spending with the target provided by the SGR. Inherent flaws in the SGR have resulted in annual cuts of 3% to 5% under this methodology. As such, an extensive amount of noise exists within the medical community about the perceived shortcomings of the SGR formula, resulting in major scrutiny by providers and regulators alike over the conversion factor and its ability to compensate physicians fairly for services. Usually, Congress steps in and issues a "doc fix" to avert payment cuts by artificial reduction, and even in some years affected an overall increase. For example, the 2013 published rule (i.e., conversion factor taking SGR into account) was $25.0008. Congress overturned this and issued the "doc fix" value at $34.0230.

The conversion factor is derived in essence from myriad sources, including the calculations and overall foundations established for deriving SGR (and ultimately the conversion factor) but overlaid by simple politics.

Medicare reimbursement is based on individual CPT code determination and derived by totaling RVUs for the service, then multiplying by the conversion factor. The geographic adjustment factor (GAF) is another layer in the process. This is supposed to account for cost differences from one geographic area within the United States to another. It is based on the cost of living in various places and other socioeconomic and environmental characteristics. The reimbursement for a given CPT code is determined by taking the total RVUs for the service and multiplying by the conversion factor. Furthermore, the GAF, also known as the geographic practice cost indices (GPCI), is applied to consider cost differences from one area of the country to another. The method for determining Medicare reimbursement is given below for a level four emergency E&M services in 2013 (i.e., CPT code 99284):

$$\{(wRVUs \times Work\ GPCI) + (Practice\ Expense\ RVUs \times PE\ GPCI) +$$
$$(Liability\ Insurance\ RVUs \times PLI\ GPCI)\} = Total\ RVUs \times Conversion$$
$$Factor = Medicare\ Payment$$
$$(2.56)(1.000) + (0.58)(0.912) + (0.22)(0.809) = 3.26694$$
$$(Total\ RVUs)\ (Conversion\ Factor) = Medicare\ Payment$$
$$(3.26694)\ (\$34.0230) = \$111.1511$$

Later in this book, we delve into this dynamic situation and provide more in-depth examples of such calculations and their derivatives of reimbursement.

With RVUs defined and their foundation of being a part of the U.S. government's (i.e., CMS) reimbursement structure and calculations, let us look at more history and background pertaining to RVUs, particularly as they can be used within the medical practice for measuring provider productivity and evaluating costs of that productivity.

RVU USES

In considering the history and background of RVUs, it is important early on to note their uses. In addition to being a source for reimbursement and in essence payment to providers (vis-à-vis, the RBRVS system), RVUs have a very important, perhaps even essential use in practice management. A major area of consideration is the fact that they are a methodology for measuring productivity, as discussed earlier in the context of differing forms of productivity. As such, RVUs comprise a major contributor to measuring and evaluating provider productivity. Particularly with respect to newer payment models starting to arise (e.g., medical homes, bundled payments, etc.), productivity, and by extension, RVUs, will continue to play a pivotal role in determining provider reimbursement. Regardless of us moving into an era where non-productivity measures, such as quality and patient outcomes, factor into compensation structures, productivity-based payments (fee for service) will continue to exist. As we further explore characteristics of RVUs, we will spend extensive time on this subject.

RVUs have continued to form a basis for costs analysis. The ability for a practice to consider its costs of services on a per-unit (RVU) basis is extremely valuable. Once the practice knows its average collected revenue per RVU, it can then subtract costs per RVU to derive an operating margin.

RVUs also have remained useful in practice management as a benchmarking source. Most of the major surveys such as the Medical Group Management Association (MGMA), the American Medical Group Association (AMGA), and others use RVUs as a major benchmarking standard. Moreover, benchmarking using RVUs can be completed by the specific practice internally, especially if they have accumulated RVU data historically. If historical RVU data have not been collected, it is relatively easy to retroactively retrieve this information. All RVU values are derived from CPT code utilization, which all practices should maintain historically.

Also within the practice, RVUs have become and remain a great source for resource allocation, particularly in two major areas: provider compensation and managed care contracting. Chapter 4 will examine closely RVUs and compensation; thus, we will not discuss it here. Because of their value as the basis for reimbursement by the government (Medicare/Medicaid), RVUs are also a valuable resource for preparing for and completing contract negotiations. As we mentioned earlier, commercial payers throughout the nation use Medicare's rates to establish their own contract rates. Contingent on market competition, these rates can range anywhere from 150% or more to less than 100% of the Medicare rates. One of the main opportunities of RVUs is their extreme influence on physician reimbursement and, thereby, financial stability. Nonetheless, the ability to reap the full benefit of this opportunity comes from the organization's ability to properly negotiate payer contracts. Smaller practices might be caught short in this process if they do not have the proper resources or expertise to negotiate fair contracts, and as such, fair conversion factors. However, as we will discuss in Chapter 3, partnering tactics such as alignment has afforded the medical community with several strategies for pooling resources, transferring contracting responsibilities, and using RVUs to take full advantage of the several opportunities brought about by the accountable care era.

RVU LIMITATIONS

Up to this point, we have reviewed several ways in which RVUs are a positive and valuable tool for medical practice. However, it is important to note that RVUs, like most measurement tools, have limitations, and taking these into account when utilizing RVUs will only perpetuate good management.

First, RVUs are not meant to provide adjustments for risks or case severity. They are not used to determine compliance in coding and documentation. In fact, when RVUs are used as a measurement for compensation to the providers, there must be a very strong and reliable compliance plan in place to ensure accurate coding practice. RVUs are not a diagnostic tool to determine the medical assessment of the patient.

Second, while RVUs are payer blind, they do not consider the reality of cash coming into the practice. In some situations where RVUs are relied on greatly as a measure of productivity, somewhat of a disregard for the reality of "real money" gives rise to mismanagement. In other words, at the end of any process of analysis, whether it be performance or productivity, costs or bottom line, there must be the utilization and consideration of actual dollars received and expended, not just RVUs. Although most practices adhere to the standard of a dollar-based financial analysis, they can become too enamored with RVUs and lose track of, or worse yet ignore, actual dollars as opposed to the RVUs.

Lastly, RVUs have yet to consider quality of care and clinical outcomes, which are becoming increasingly interesting in reimbursement matters.[4] Moreover, RVUs do not measure practice efficiencies nor do they provide any insights as to

---

[4]In 2013, CMS approved of new CPT codes assigned to care management services, and accepted the RUC's RVU recommendations for the same, indicating a shift in RVU applications to the quality realm.

why a practice is operating efficiently or not. (A possible exception to this would be a high cost per RVU that could lead to the conclusion of an inefficient practice operation.)

OTHER UNIT MEASUREMENTS

This book focuses primarily on relative value units as a basis for managing the practice, yet other similar standards have continued to be used to measure productivity and costs. Time relative value unit (Time RVU) is of greater significance and applicability in some settings. This is especially applicable and used as a system for the valuation of dental procedures and the development of dental fees [also called a relative time-cost unit (RTCU) system]. However, this also applies to medical practices such as cardiology practices where Time RVUs may be a fairer method of productivity and cost assessment than RVUs. Also, anesthesia has many individual and unique characteristics that have led to some specific applications for these specialists. Likewise, pathology has developed some of its own unique characteristics within the system. These special cases will be addressed as we continue to explore the entire subject in greater detail.

CONCLUSION

Since their adoption into the medical world by CMS over 20 years ago, RVUs have remained the primary vehicle for productivity measurement in medical practice, and the CMS standard for reimbursement. Throughout their tenure, they have provided greater insights into the value of medical services being performed, and they inherently consider variances in the resources needed versus those actually consumed by providers when rendering professional services. While they have certain limitations, the RVU system is arguably the best methodology available for performance management in the medical, and in some cases, healthcare practice.

The next chapter will address CMS and RVU considerations as they stand today.

CMS and RVU Considerations

While RVUs do not work exclusively for the benefit of the Centers for Medicare and Medicaid Services (CMS), this governing body holds substantial weight when it comes to defining the value and use of RVUs. First and foremost, CMS plays a large role in determining the value associated with RVUs. It also uses the resource-based relative value scale (RBRVS) to reimburse healthcare providers for the services they provide to healthcare participants. In this chapter, we further explore these two components to the RVU continuum.

ESTABLISHING RVU VALUES

The Relative Value Scale Update Committee (RUC) was introduced in the previous chapter. This committee plays an important role in establishing the physician work component of RVUs (wRVUs). RUC works closely with the CPT Editorial Panel to develop recommendations for changes to existing CPT codes and additions of new codes. Supporting the CPT Editorial Panel in its work is a larger body of CPT advisors: the CPT Advisory Committee. While RUC does not have the authority to modify the CPT codes, there is a long history of CMS largely accepting the RUC's recommendations.

Prior to reviewing some of the changes that have occurred with the RUC and CMS working together, it is important to put RUC into context with regard to its members. New codes or changes to existing codes originate with the CPT Editorial Panel. Essentially, various specialty societies make recommendations to the CPT Editorial Panel whose members then decide to reject the proposed addition/change, put the addition/change on hold, or recommend the addi-tion/change to the RUC. The CPT Editorial Panel is comprised of 17 members, 13 of whom are nominated by the American Medical Association; the remaining four seats are occupied by individuals nominated by each of the following:

- Blue Cross and Blue Shield Association (BCBS)
- Health Insurance Association of America (HIAA)
- CMS
- American Hospital Association (AHA)

Once the CPT Editorial Panel recommends a change/addition for a CPT code, the RUC then comes into play. The RUC is comprised of 31 members with the 2 latest additions announced in February 2012. The majority of these members (21) represent major national medical societies. The societies represented have a large percentage of physicians in patient care and also account for a large portion of Medicare patients. Four seats rotate on a two-year basis. One seat is reserved for a primary care representative; two are reserved for an internal medicine subspecialist; and the fourth is open to any other specialty society not a member of the RUC, except internal medicine or primary care representatives. The remaining six seats are held by the following individuals:

- RUC Chair
- Co-Chair of the RUC Health Care Professionals Advisory Committee (HCPAC) Review Board
- American Medical Association Representative
- American Osteopathic Association Representative
- Chair of the Practice Expense Subcommittee
- Chair of the CPT Editorial Panel

The specialties represented include the following:

Anesthesiology	Ophthalmology
Cardiology	Orthopedic Surgery
Cardiothoracic Surgery	Otolaryngology
Dermatology	Pathology
Emergency Medicine	Pediatrics
Family Medicine	Plastic Surgery
General Surgery	Primary Care*
Geriatric Medicine	Psychiatry
Infectious Disease*	Radiology
Internal Medicine	Rheumatology*
Neurology	Urology
Neurosurgery	Vascular Surgery*
Obstetrics/Gynecology	(*Indicates rotating seat)

As the above list indicates, there is a good cross-section of specialties listed with a solid differentiation between primary care, internal medicine subspecialties, and surgical specialties.

While RUC performs reviews on an annual basis, its main function is the five-year review. This first occurred in 1997, with the second in 2000, the third in 2005, and the fourth occurring in 2010. As noted above, the RUC does not have authority to change CPT codes independent of CMS, but CMS has a long history of accepting the RUC's recommendations. Specifically, in 1995, the RUC made recommendations on more than 1,100 codes and CMS accepted 95% of their recommendations and implemented them in 1997. In 2002, recommendations from the 2000 review were submitted on more than 850 codes and there was a

98% acceptance rate by CMS. The trend continued in 2007, with CMS accepting 97% of the proposed changes on approximately 750 codes. And for the fourth review in 2010, almost 300 codes were recommended with 75% accepted by CMS and implemented January 1, 2012. Accordingly, RUC has considerable weight in influencing the CPT code process and, in turn, the overall reimbursement process.

As noted, it is important to remember that RUC's main function is the assignment of the work component of RVUs. The separate Practice Expense Committee (PEAC), a RUC subcommittee, analyzes and makes recommendations of the practice expense component of the RVUs assigned to CPT codes.

While the practice expense component is an important part of the RVU and overall reimbursement process, much more weight and focus is placed on the wRVUs. This is because much of the focus on RVUs is measuring the productivity of physicians. The wRVU values are a much better representation of this than the other RVU components or even RVUs in total.

It is not necessary to analyze all of the historical changes RUC has made to RVUs, but it is worth mentioning the results of the most recent fourth five-year review process. While 290 CPT codes were submitted with work relative value recommendations ranging from increasing, decreasing, or maintaining the relative values, CMS accepted 75% of the RUC's recommendations.

To illustrate, Table 2-1 presents the most recent changes associated with the E&M codes. These are the codes that have a high level of volume across the majority of specialties. Essentially, overnight the wRVU value associated with these E&M codes increased on average just below 6%. These changes, along with all the other changes included in the five-year review process, were a result of the RUC's recommendations. This level of increase in wRVU values increases the total RVUs associated with this code, which then increases reimbursement. The changes also impact the productivity of physicians who are paid via a wRVU plan (which we will explore in Chapter 3).

TABLE 2-1	Examples of E&M Code Changes				
		wRVU		wRVU Change	% Change
CPT Code	Description	2010	2009		
99201	Office/outpatient visit, new	0.48	0.45	0.03	6.67%
99202	Office/outpatient visit, new	0.93	0.88	0.05	5.68%
99203	Office/outpatient visit, new	1.42	1.34	0.08	5.97%
99204	Office/outpatient visit, new	2.43	2.3	0.13	5.65%
99205	Office/outpatient visit, new	3.17	3	0.17	5.67%
99211	Office/outpatient visit, established	0.18	0.17	0.01	5.88%
99212	Office/outpatient visit, established	0.48	0.45	0.03	6.67%
99213	Office/outpatient visit, established	0.97	0.92	0.05	5.43%
99214	Office/outpatient visit, established	1.5	1.42	0.08	5.63%
99215	Office/outpatient visit, established	2.11	2	0.11	5.50%

This information is important as it indicates that RVUs, and especially wRVUs, are not a constant, but are subject to change. As discussed in Chapter 1, many view their stability as one of the benefits of using RVUs as opposed to other metrics. This is still true for the most part. However, the changes that occurred for the E&M codes in 2007 were atypical with greater than 10% increases. Changes of this magnitude are uncommon in years where there is not a five-year review. Accordingly, the most often a user has to worry about substantial changes to RVUs is every five years. Oftentimes, these changes can go relatively unpublicized to the typical healthcare professional. In fact, many employed physician networks t h a t compensate their physicians using a work RVU model were unaware of the 2007 changes prior to them becoming effective. As a result, compensation plans paid their physicians substantially more compensation for no true increases in work.

As a simple example, consider a physician who generated 4,500 wRVUs in 2006. In 2007, he saw the exact same patients, generated the exact same level of collections, but due to the wRVU value changes, generated 5,310 work RVUs—an 18% increase. Assuming, in both years he receives $40.00 per work RVU generated as compensation, this would equate to a $32,400 increase in 2007 for the same level of work. As collections did not increase, the hospital just increased its overhead by a substantial amount. The hospital could have resolved this issue simply by recalibrating the compensation plan by lowering the compensation rate per wRVU.

As many employed physician networks did not realize the changes until after the fact, they already had paid out substantial amounts of additional compensation and still had to go in and recalibrate their plan. (We discuss work RVUs and compensation later in this book.)

Still, RVU values do change from time to time, and there is a solid methodology for modifying them. Anyone who uses RVUs for evaluating productivity and for compensation purposes must be cognizant of these changes and proactively adjust their use based on any changes that occur. This is a critical issue that sometimes may be overlooked.

REIMBURSING PHYSICIANS FOR THEIR SERVICES

The primary purpose of the RBRVS was not to develop a system that merely provides data for the sake of providing data. Rather, it was designed as a system in which describing, quantifying, and reimbursing physician services could be made relative to one another. There is a common misconception that RBRVS pertain only to Medicare patients since CMS funded and instigated the original study in evaluating the resources and costs associated with delivery of physician services. While it is used by CMS for Medicare reimbursement, many third-party payers have adopted the RBRVS as their payment methodology, essentially piggybacking on the government's efforts. It is evident that this is the case by the fact that representatives of BCBS and the HIAA sit on the CPT Editorial Panel.

To review, the following is the standard CMS reimbursement calculation, inclusive of all the varying components.

$$=[(\text{Work RVU*Work GPCI})^1+$$
$$(\text{Facility or Non- Facility Practice Expense RVU}\ *$$
$$\text{Practice Expense GPCI}) +$$
$$(\text{Malpractice Expense RVU}\ *$$
$$\text{Malpractice Expense GPCI})]$$

While the RVU values change frequently, the main way CMS influences reimbursement is by modifying the conversion factor. For 2013, the Medicare conversion factor is $34.0230. Thus, Total RVUs are multiplied by $34.0230 to determine reimbursement for any procedure. While the calculation to get to Total RVUs can be somewhat complex due to the three different components and the geographic adjustments associated with each, once Total RVUs are derived, the remainder of the calculation is very straightforward.

As mentioned, many third-party payers use the RBRVS for reimbursement methodology. Essentially, they maintain the integrity of all the RVU values and adjust the conversion factor. This is typically done based on a percentage of the Medicare conversion factor. For example, in a certain geographical area, BCBS may reimburse at 115% of Medicare. Thus, their effective conversion factor is $39.1265 ($34.0230 x 115%). This conversion factor would then be multiplied by Total RVUs to derive the reimbursement for BCBS patients.

CONCLUSION

There is well-established methodology for developing and revising RVU values. Much thought goes into the RVUs assigned to each CPT code so they properly reflect the complexity, risk, time, and expense associated with the procedure performed and are aligned from one CPT code to another. There will always be differing opinions regarding the RVU values assigned and the overall reimbursement methodology. No system is perfect, but the RBRVS continues to build on a long history of acceptance in the healthcare industry.

Now that a solid foundation regarding the history of RVUs and their maintenance and interaction with CMS has been established, the remainder of the chapters will analyze various uses of RVUs throughout the medical practice.

---

[1] Geographic Practice Cost Index used to reflect the variations in the cost of providing services between different geographic areas. There are different GPCT's for work, practice expense, and malpractice.

The Effect of RVUs on Physician/ Hospital Alignment

The impact of RVUs is increasing in a number of different areas, including hospital/ physician alignment. This chapter provides an overview of the alignment market and the areas wherein RVUs are having an impact.

OVERVIEW OF ALIGNMENT MARKET

One word to describe the current healthcare market is "consolidation." While consolidation is occurring in many facets of the industry, a key area is within physician practices. Due to a variety of factors, physicians are choosing to exit private practice and becoming employees of or affiliated/integrated in some way with hospitals. The opportunities for alignment vary greatly and range from what is considered a low level of integration to full integration. Although RVUs do not affect all of these areas of alignment, they are prevalent in some, shaping the way the alignment transaction occurs or driving the reason for alignment.

SPECIFIC ALIGNMENT MODELS

Figure 3-1 outlines a variety of alignment models, indicating the level of alignment, the specific strategy and concept, as well as the compensation framework within that particular model.

Each of these alignment models is occurring within the industry to varying degrees. As a general rule, RVUs are impacted more by the higher levels of alignment/ integration than the lower levels. The following section highlights areas where alignment is impacted by RVUs.

RVUS WITHIN ALIGNMENT MODELS

As highlighted above, alignment is occurring at a rapid pace. Not all alignment models have an element of RVUs, but many do. Further, the way RVUs impact alignment varies greatly in terms of both function and scope. We explore the key areas where alignment has been impacted by RVUs below.

	FIGURE 3-1	Comparisons of Alignment Models	
Level of Alignment	**Strategy**	**Basic Concept**	**Compensation Framework**
Low	Managed Care Networks (IPAs, PHOs)	• Loosely formed alliances • Primarily for contracting purposes • Limited in ability unless clinically integrated • Being used as a platform for ACO development	• No true impact on pay unless through improved payer contracts • If used as platform for ACO, could result in distribution of incentives received
Low	Call Coverage Stipends	• Compensation for the personal, financial, and risk burden associated with ED coverage	• Payment can come in the form of a daily stipend, fee for service payment, or hybrid payment • Could be paid via wRVU credit within employment
Low	Medical Directorships	• Payment for defined administrative services • Must be a true need for the services	• Typically paid via a market-based hourly rate • Could be paid with wRVU credit within employment
Low	Recruitment/ Incubation	• Traditional style of a hospital financially supporting a new recruit	• Allows existing physicians in practice to not see a decrease in their pay as a new physician comes on board
Medium	Management Services (MSO)	• Services such as revenue cycle, human resources, IT, etc. • Can be hospital-owned, joint venture, private practice owned	• Can provide an additional revenue stream
Medium	Equity Model Assimilation	• Ties all entities via legal agreements • Can jointly contract with payers	• Can result in increased profitability through better payer contracts and other efficiencies
Medium	Target Cost Objectives	• Focus to ensure delivery of cost-effective care while still maintaining quality	• Savings shared with providers • Percentage • Hourly fee • Fixed fee
Medium	Provider Equity (Joint ventures, investments)	• Joint ventures such as specialty hospitals, surgery centers, etc.	• Can provide an additional revenue stream to private practice physicians
Medium	Clinical Co-Management/ Service Line Management	• Provision of administrative services and work toward certain strategic initiatives within a service line	• Involves hourly payment for administrative time and incentive payment for achieving established metrics
High	Employment	• Traditional employment arrangement with a hospital	• Typically includes productivity payment and potentially some other incentives for quality, cost control • In a majority of situations, models include a wRVU-based compensation methodology

FIGURE 3-1 Comparisons of Alignment Models			
Level of Alignment	**Strategy**	**Basic Concept**	**Compensation Framework**
High	Employment Lite (PSA model)	• Allows practice to remain private, but hedge payer risk • Hospital owns receivables	• Hospital provides payment, often-times on wRVU basis, which is intended to provide FMV compensation, benefits, and other overhead costs incurred by practice

- ***Reductions in RVU Values.*** One factor associated with RVUs that has driven alignment is the reduction in RVU values for certain procedures. The change in wRVU values for certain cardiology codes is a great example. Table 3-1 highlights the changes in certain cardiology CPT codes from 2007 to 2013. Note that many of these codes did not exist in 2013, but the procedures were represented by other codes that were "bundled" into the current codes, which have existed for the past several years.

  Some of these codes represent a significant portion of work that cardiologists perform, especially on the ancillary side of the equation. Further, the physicians invested in expensive equipment to be able to perform these procedures in the office. These decreases in wRVU values, which ultimately decreased overall reimbursement, have had a significant impact on revenue and, in turn, compensation. As a result, many cardiologists have given up private practice and become employed by healthcare systems. Thus, a key driver of alignment deals, especially in the cardiology arena, has been a result of the changing wRVU values.

- ***Use in Professional Services Agreement (PSA) Models.*** Another area where RVUs have had a significant impact in terms of alignment has been in PSA alignment models. These are often called "employment lite." The PSA model has many characteristics of the employment model but stops significantly short of employment in various ways and areas. Under such settings, the hospital engages the physicians' practice to provide services for that service line.

TABLE 3-1 Reductions in RVUs for Certain Cardiology Codes					
CPT Code	**Description**	**2007**	**2013**	**Change**	**% Change**
78451	Ht muscle image spect sing	1.89	1.38	(0.51)	–27%
78452	Ht muscle image spect mult	2.26	1.62	(0.64)	–28%
93306	Tte w/doppler complete	1.37	1.30	(0.07)	–5%
93458	L hrt artery/ventricle angio	6.65	5.85	(0.80)	–12%
93459	L hrt art/grft angio	7.48	6.60	(0.88)	–12%
93460	R&l hrt art/ventricle angio	8.31	7.35	(0.96)	–12%

Specifically, consider the following elements of this approach:

— The comprehensive alignment strategy has characteristics of employment, but stops short of and requires less integration.

— The hospital engages the practice to provide comprehensive professional services through a PSA.

— The hospital establishes fee schedules and negotiates payer contracts; the practice's professional services are billed under the hospital's tax ID.

— The practice acts as an independent contractor to the hospital and invoices for professional services rendered (1099 status); the practice's legal and tax structure remain intact.

— The practice is compensated directly from the hospital via a global fee.

— Global fee rates are calculated based on annual budgeted amount for overhead and work RVU for provider compensation (wRVU).

— The global fee rate can be broken down into various components to separately address professional services (the physician fee component) and practice expenses (the overhead component).

— Sometimes, a global fee rate that includes both overhead and physician fee components is requested; the hospital may prefer these components be separately negotiated and paid.

— The practice remains responsible for maintaining its staff, benefits, compensation, and tax filing; these costs are reimbursed to the practice via the overhead component of the global fee.

— The practice remains responsible for physician compensation, benefits, and tax filing; these costs are reimbursed to the practice via the physician fee component of the global fee.

— All rates are pre-negotiated and must be consistent with FMV/commercially reasonable.

Four PSA Model Structures

The following summarizes four distinctive PSA model characteristics and clearly explains the major differentiators.

1. Hospital contracts with practice for global payment; practice retains all management responsibilities (global payment PSA).
   - Practice is an independent contractor.
   - Physicians still "employed" by practice.
   - Self-employed status—no benefits from hospital.
   - Practice invoices hospital for actual services rendered (usually in wRVUs, converted to dollars).
   - Hospital pays practice directly without any withholding.
   - Hospital files 1099 with IRS showing what they paid the practice/physicians; practice is responsible for withholding taxes from physician.

2. Hospital employs physicians; practice retained and contracts with hospital to provide administrative management—staff not employed by hospital.

- Physicians employed (W-2).
- Management contracted with practice.
- Management infrastructure retained by practice.
- Staff employed by practice.
- This mirrors the practice management arrangement explained above.

3. Hospital contracts with practice for its physicians to provide professional services; hospital employs staff and "owns" administrative structure (traditional PSA).
   - Practice is an independent contractor that then employs physicians.
   - Staff employed by hospital(s).
   - Administrative infrastructure owned and provided by the hospital(s).
   - Hospital pays the practice 1099 fees for professional services.

4. Hospital employs/contracts with practice physicians; practice spun-off into a jointly-owned (hospital and practice) MSO/ISO.
   - Hospital(s) employs or contracts with practice.
   - Jointly-owned (hospital(s) and practice) management and IT organization (MSO, ISO).
   - MSO/ISO contracts for management services with hospital(s).

Typically, PSA models #1 and #3 above (global pay and traditional, respectively) are the most popular, with models #2 and #4 hybrids of these two. These two main models are visually illustrated below in Figure 3-2 and Figure 3-3.

Within PSA models, wRVUs come into play in two key areas.

- **Professional services rate per wRVU**: This rate is set in a manner similar to the way it is set in an employment arrangement (see Chapter 4). The key

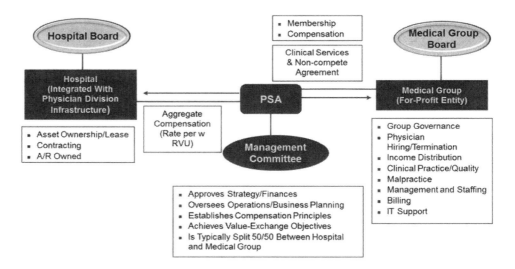

FIGURE 3-2 Illustrative Example of Global Payment PSA Model

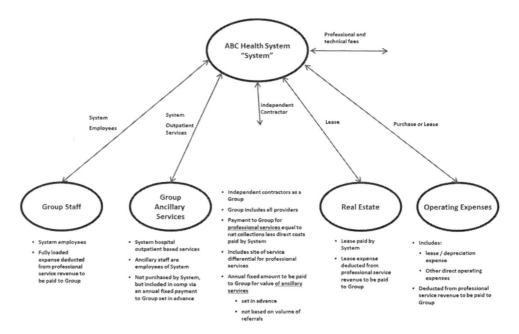

FIGURE 3-3   Illustrative Example of Traditional PSA Model

difference is that this rate tends to be "grossed up" for benefits. However, benefits could also be treated as an overhead item. In a PSA model, the per-wRVU payment typically represents the totality of compensation for professional services. Thus, while still private, the hospital is managing the professional fee revenue cycle and simply is "subscribing" to the practice's professional services and paying for such via the rate per wRVU.

- **Variable Overhead Rate per wRVU:** Outside the professional services rate per wRVU, the other area where RVUs are used is in the reimbursement of variable overhead. While fixed overhead is often paid at a fixed monthly amount, the variable overhead is often tied to productivity. There are two approaches:

  —*Baseline with Rate for Excess Production:* The first approach is to include a portion of the variable overhead reimbursement within the fixed over-head payment. In this instance, variable overhead is not paid until pro-ductivity exceeds a certain threshold, typically the historical productivity level of the practice that coincides with the overhead value. The thought is that the historical overhead of the practice captures this variable overhead until this point. Thus, only when productivity exceeds certain levels is variable overhead paid in addition.

  An example of this is a practice that historically incurred $150,000 in variable overhead. If the historical fixed overhead was $2,250,000, then the full overhead payment would be $2,400,000. If historical productiv-ity was 44,000 for the practice, then the variable overhead rate totals $3.41 per wRVU. Thus, only when productivity exceeds 44,000 would this additional overhead rate be paid.

—*Rate for All Production:* In this situation, the fixed overhead and variable overhead reimbursement are split from the onset. Thus, using the above example, the fixed overhead payment would total $2,250,000 and then all wRVUs would be paid at $3.41 to recognize the variable overhead.

As many practices realize the need to make some change, but do not want to move fully to employment, the PSA model has provided a nice middle ground wherein there is a much stronger alignment between the hospital and practice, but all autonomy is not lost. In many cases, the PSA model is viewed as an interim step for three to five years between private practice and full employment.

- **wRVU Credit in Lieu of an Hourly Rate.** RVUs also play a role in other components of a compensation arrangement, outside of the professional clinical services component. For example, many employment arrangements require the physicians to perform certain medical director activities, go to outreach sites, provide excess call coverage, etc. Historically, the main way to compensate for these activities was through an hourly rate or daily stipend. However, many health systems use a single payment methodology; therefore, instead of compensating professional services via wRVUs and medical director or other activities by other means, they provide wRVU credit for these other activities. For instance, a medical director may receive 2.5 wRVUs for every hour of medical director work performed. Or, a physician performing outreach work may be guaranteed no fewer than 20 wRVUs per day. Thus, if the outreach volume is less than what the physician can normally generate, he is not penalized.

   In other instances, health systems are developing a proxy wRVU system to measure physician activity in certain areas even if it does not directly impact the compensation plan. This may be done to gain a better understanding of a physician's overall contributions or for compliance purposes.

Although not directly correlated, the use of wRVUs has accelerated alongside the uptick in alignment and the use is more than in the basic wRVU-based compensation arrangement within employment.

RVUS AND QUALITY INCENTIVE ARRANGEMENTS

More and more physician compensation arrangements involve an element of quality incentives. Quality incentives alone have nothing to do with RVUs, but indirectly, the quality incentives are affecting the structure of how RVUs are used in physician compensation arrangements.

The first way in which RVUs are impacted is in the value of the RVU component of the compensation arrangement. Historically, it was common for 100% of compensation to be tied to wRVU-based compensation. This is no longer the case. Now, the wRVU-based component is representing about 70% to 95% of the compensation arrangement, with the remainder often tied to quality. As it does not make sense to simply add more compensation to the arrangement by including the quality incentive, the wRVU-based incentive must be scaled down. Table 3-2 shows a simple example of this concept.

TABLE 3-2 WRVU-BASED INCENTIVE COMPENSATION EXAMPLE		
	Yesterday	**Today**
Base Compensation	$250,000	$225,000
Productivity Incentive Per wRVU	$40.00	$36.00
At 6,500 wRVUs	$260,000	$234,000
Quality Incentive	$0	$25,000
Total Compensation	$260,000	$259,000

In the example, the Yesterday column represents a model that was 100% based on wRVU productivity. If a physician generated 6,500 wRVUs, the total compensation would be $260,000—$250,000 of base and $10,000 of actual productivity incentive. There is no quality incentive in this example. In the Today column, the productivity incentive rate per wRVU, or conversion factor, is reduced by $4.00 and a potential quality incentive is added. Thus, in this example if a physician generated 6,500 wRVUs, the productivity-based compensation would be $234,000—$225,000 in base compensation and $9,000 in productivity incentive. Then, there is a $25,000 quality incentive resulting in total compensation of $259,000. Thus, the total compensation is similar, but its composition is very different. This concept is becoming more and more the norm, which is diluting the effect of RVUs in the compensation arrangement.

Another key way RVUs are being affected by the quality incentive is in terms of how the actual RVU model is structured. In the above example, the quality incentive is simply added to the RVU-based arrangement, but in other instances, the RVU-based model is impacted in other ways. One of these is through the use of a variable rate per wRVU.

A variable rate per wRVU means the rate per wRVU fluctuates with performance in certain areas. Figure 3-4 illustrates to examples.

In this first example, the rate is set at two and 15% ($6.00) of the rate is tied to non-productivity criteria. If the physician achieves only 80% of the non-productivity criteria, the ultimate rate per wRVU applied would total $38.80. In example two, the full rate will be tied to the quality incentives. Thus, if 80% is achieved here, the ultimate rate is much lower, at $32.00.

Clearly, this approach provides much more focus on the quality initiatives and ties the quality and productivity together. This means full benefit is achieved only

FIGURE 3-4 EXAMPLES OF WRVU FLUCTUATIONS BASED ON PERFORMANCE	
Example One	**Example Two**
Fully Loaded Rate: $40.00	Fully Loaded Rate: $40.00
Amount tied to Non-Productivity: 15% ($6.00)	Amount tied to Non-Productivity: 100% ($40.00)
Achievement of Non-Productivity Incentives: 80%	Achievement of Non-Productivity Incentives: 80%
Ultimate Rate: $38.80	Ultimate Rate: $32.00

with reasonable productivity levels that are generated with high levels of quality; without one or the other, full benefit does not accrue to the physician.

There are some challenges with this approach. For example, if base compensation is guaranteed and no productivity incentive is earned, this approach has little impact. In other words, if a physician is not negatively affected by a lower rate per wRVU, the model is impotent. Additionally, some physicians believe there should not be just negative consequences for poor performance, but also incentives for high performance (the carrot vs. stick concept). With this in mind, one approach would be to establish the base rate per wRVU at $34.00 and provide the opportunity to get up to $40.00. Thus, it is all a matter of perspective.

SUMMARY

The information presented in this chapter highlights a number of ways RVUs are affecting the hospital/physician alignment process. This ranges from basic wRVU-based compensation models in employment, as is further discussed in Chapter 4, to their use in PSA arrangements, to their effect on quality incentives as well as the continued use of proxy wRVU methodologies. Regardless of the alignment structure, being able to track a physician's activity will always be important and, therefore, RVUs will likely continue to play a key role.

RVUs and Compensation

In recent years, the use of wRVUs has become the main measure of productivity within the industry. This is more so the case in hospital employment, but their use continues to gain ground in private practice as well. As discussed in Chapter 1, there are other productivity metrics out there that are still being used, but none to the extent of wRVUs. In some instances, collections are still used as a measure of productivity in hospital employment, but the occurrences are limited. Other measures of productivity, such as gross charges, are practically never used, despite their historical significance. The main reason gross charges are no longer used is that each healthcare entity has the liberty to set its fee schedule however it chooses and it can be modified from time to time. Thus, if a physician is compensated on gross charges and the fee schedule increases, the physician automatically gets a raise if the compensation plan is not recalibrated. Collections also have been used heavily in the past and continue to be the most predominant productivity measure used in private practice. However, they are used less frequently in hospital-employed settings. This is because physicians do not have much, if any, influence over their payer mix, and they do not personally control the efficiency of the billing office. Thus, they can be performing all of the work they possibly can, but whether they receive payment for those services is largely out of their control.

Due to the challenges associated with using gross charges and collections, as noted above, the focus has turned to using RVUs in both the private practice and hospital-employed settings, although they are used in rather different manners. In terms of compensation, wRVUs are used more often as opposed to the other RVU components. This is because the wRVU component is based completely on the work that the physicians are actually performing, which for purposes of compensation should be the key focus.

In this chapter we explore how wRVUs are used in private practice and in hospital-employed settings to compensate physicians.

PRIVATE PRACTICE

Private practices often operate similarly to hospital-owned practices, with one major difference: profits. In a private practice, physician compensation is constrained by the practice's profitability. Thus, to create more income, the practice can increase revenues, decrease expenses, or both. Hospital-owned settings oftentimes offer more flexibility as a larger entity (i.e., the overall health system) that can fund losses in the practice setting. Within hospital-employment, the focus is oftentimes less on profits and more on ensuring market-based compensation using a number of metrics to determine such. For a multitude of reasons, a hospital/health system may deem a loss to be acceptable within the four walls of the practice, with some limitations, of course.

Accordingly, due to the constraints of private practices in terms of compensating based on their profitability only, there is a limited amount of profit before physician expenses to work with. We deem profit before physician expenses to be collections less overhead (exclusive of any physician expenses). To illustrate further, consider Table 4-1.

While the amounts of funds to work with are limited, the various components can be allocated in a variety of ways. This is where wRVUs come into play. While other productivity measures can also be used, many view the use of wRVUs as the most objective measure. In some instances, practices choose to blend two productivity measures, such as collections and wRVUs or wRVUs and gross charges.

As an example, consider a situation wherein some services that are provided generate a sizable amount of collections, but do not have a large wRVU value. There would be a disincentive for the physicians in the practice to perform these procedures if all productivity is based on wRVUs. Accordingly, in this instance, it may make sense to blend wRVUs and collections as the productivity measure.

TABLE 4-1 Sample Profit and Loss Statement	
Collections	
Less: Refunds	
Total Revenue	
Expenses	
Personnel	
Occupancy	
Variable	
Fixed	
Total Expenses	
Profit Before Physician Expenses	
Physician Expenses	
Compensation	
Payroll Taxes	
Benefits	
Total Physician Expenses	
Net Income	

©2009 Coker Group

TABLE 4-2 Example of Blended Productivity Measures

	wRVUs		Collections		Blended
Physician A	11,297	17.02%	$1,010,120	16.07%	16.55%
Physician B	10,739	16.18%	$1,063,706	16.93%	16.55%
Physician C	9,091	13.70%	$846,732	13.47%	13.59%
Physician D	8,124	12.24%	$741,179	11.79%	12.02%
Physician E	10,428	15.71%	$914,265	14.55%	15.13%
Physician F	10,803	16.28%	$1,109,532	17.65%	16.97%
Physician G	5,880	8.86%	$599,028	9.53%	9.20%
Total	66,362	100.00%	$6,284,561	100.00%	100.00%

©2009 Coker Group

Consider the example of blended productivity measures in Table 4-2. In this example, wRVUs and collections follow a relatively similar pattern, albeit with minor differences. This scenario weights each metric by 50%, but more weight could be given to one of the measures. For instance, wRVUs could be weighted 75% to place more emphasis on them than on collections.

Another situation in which wRVUs are used largely as an allocation mechanism is in practices wherein the payer mix varies significantly between providers. For example, one provider may be located in a highly affluent area, where a favorable payer mix exists, while another may be located in a less affluent area, where Medicaid and other low-paying payers are predominant. In these situations, wRVUs can be used to level the playing field completely (i.e., allocation solely using wRVUs) or partially (i.e., allocation partially based on wRVUs) by using wRVUs to allocate revenue generated. In many instances, a partial allocation is preferred in that taking the focus completely off of payer mix within a private practice (where cash is king) can be detrimental in the long term.

In terms of deciding whether to use wRVUs only, another measure of productivity, or a blended measure of productivity, there is no right or wrong answer. None of the measures are perfect, which lends credence to blending two or more of the measures. Essentially, each practice must study their data, outline the intricacies of their practice, and determine what works best for them. For the remainder of this chapter, we will focus on strictly using wRVUs as the productivity measures.

wRVUs are used primarily as an allocation tool in private practice. Essentially, this is a means of allocating revenue and overhead to the various physicians as part of the process of determining individual physician compensation. There are limited funds to work with in private practice, thus it is merely a way of reallocating what is there. If the profit before physician expenses is $1 million, it will still be $1 million after using wRVUs; however, the amount paid to each physician may differ somewhat.

wRVUs can be used in several ways to determine physician compensation. First, they can be used by taking a bottom-line approach and simply allocating the profit before physician expense. They can also be used in a more detailed manner by allocating revenue and expense separately. Furthermore, the allocation process does not have to be completely productivity-based, but some portion can still be allocated equally. We further delve into these various alternatives below.

Bottom-Line Allocation

This allocation method closely follows the structure outlined above in the sample profit and loss statement where overhead is subtracted from collections to arrive at the pool of monies available to the physicians (i.e., profit before physician expense). This pool can be divided in a number of ways. First, a portion of the overall amount (for instance, 10%) can be left within the practice to fund future growth with the remaining portion representing the amount available to be distributed to the physicians. The remaining amount can be allocated using wRVUs. The amount can be divided equally or based strictly on productivity or some manner that is in between these two extremes. For example, the amount available for distribution could be split in two with 50% being distributed equally and the remaining 50% being distributed based on productivity. Or the percentages can be adjusted so that more of the distribution is based on productivity in order to provide a greater incentive to produce. In most cases, we recommend that at least 75% be allocated based on productivity with no more than 25% being allocated equally. Providing an incentive for individual productivity is of utmost importance; thus, it should be the primary focus. However, in a private practice, much can be said about maintaining a cohesive group; it is important, therefore, to recognize this by sharing a portion of the distribution pool equally.

To illustrate this model, consider Table 4-3. In this example, profit before physician expense totals $3,800,000 and 25% of the profit before physician expense is shared equally. As there are seven physicians, this totals $135,714 ($3,800,000 x25% / 7). The remaining 75% of compensation is based on the physicians' wRVU productivity. For example, for Physician A, who generated 17.02% of the wRVUs in the practice, his productivity portion of the profit before physician expense

TABLE 4-3   Sample Bottom Line Allocation

Physician	wRVUs		Equal 25.00%	Production 75.00%	Total 100.00%
Physician A	11,297	17.02%	$135,714	$485,070	$620,784
Physician B	10,739	16.18%	$135,714	$461,130	$596,844
Physician C	9,091	13.70%	$135,714	$390,450	$526,164
Physician D	8,124	12.24%	$135,714	$348,840	$484,554
Physician E	10,428	15.71%	$135,714	$447,735	$583,449
Physician F	10,803	16.28%	$135,714	$463,980	$599,694
Physician G	5,880	8.87%	$135,714	$252,795	$388,509
	66,362	100.00%	$950,000	$2,850,000	$3,800,000

is calculated by multiplying 17.02% by 75% of $3,800,000, or $2,850,000. These figures, $135,714 and $485,070, are then added to achieve total compensation of $620,784. It is important to note that this figure is intended to represent the total expenses of the physician, meaning benefits are included in this figure. As an alternative, if benefit costs are rather similar across all physicians, this can be included as an overhead expense wherein the calculation ultimately results in cash compensation.

Revenue/Expense Allocation

Oftentimes, the above calculation is viewed as too basic and a more detailed calculation is desired that treats revenue and expenses separately. This is also possible to effect using wRVUs. While the bottom line allocation method performs the income distribution after overhead has been subtracted from expenses, the revenue/expense allocation method distributes all collections based on set criteria and all overhead based on set criteria. Ultimately, the same amount of monies is distributed, but this method provides more flexibility in the distribution process.

In many cases, wRVUs are used for both the revenue and expense allocation, but practice expense RVUs potentially could be used to allocate overhead. Oftentimes, wRVU data are easier to obtain, which is why it is more frequently used; but, access to RVU data, in general, is becoming less of a problem as more and more practices adopt robust practice management and electronic health records systems. In terms of allocating revenue and expenses using wRVUs, a complete productivity-based approach can be taken where both revenue and expenses are allocated based on each provider's pro rata share of productivity. Alternatively, some portion of revenue and expenses can be shared equally. In fact, we typically recommend allocating some equally and the amount differs for revenue and expenses.

With revenue, the main reason to allocate some equally is to further develop group cohesion and also account for issues when wRVUs may not perfectly allocate collections. For example, if there is a physician who is performing a high wRVU value procedure that requires very little time, while the other physicians in the group are doing the more bread and butter work, it may be necessary to share some revenues equally to account for this. Accordingly, the actual percentage of revenue/collections to share equally will vary from practice to practice, but as a general rule, 10% to 25% should be appropriate. Thus, the remaining collections are allocated based on wRVU productivity. Alternatively, as outlined above, multiple productivity measures can be weighted together.

With regard to overhead expenses, if the practice is trying to allocate these costs based on the consumption of resources, allocating fully on productivity or fully equally will not do the trick from an accounting perspective. This is because a large majority of the costs in a medical practice are fixed, wherein they remain relatively consistent regardless of the productivity level. For example, there is a basic level of staffing necessary to function, as well as space, technology, equipment, etc. Of course, at some point, the practice will have to add support staff if the physicians are extremely productive; but for the most part, many of the costs are stable. The remaining costs, such as medical supplies, transcription costs,

TABLE 4-4	Sample Revenue/Expense Allocation						
			Revenue		Expenses		
Physician	wRVUs		Equal	Production	Equal	Production	Total
Physician A	11,297	17.02%	$135,000	$911,421	($214,286)	($170,200)	$661,935
Physician B	10,739	16.18%	$135,000	$866,439	($214,286)	($161,800)	$625,353
Physician C	9,091	13.70%	$135,000	$733,635	($214,286)	($137,000)	$517,349
Physician D	8,124	12.24%	$135,000	$655,452	($214,286)	($122,400)	$453,766
Physician E	10,428	15.71%	$135,000	$841,271	($214,286)	($157,100)	$604,885
Physician F	10,803	16.28%	$135,000	$871,794	($214,286)	($162,800)	$629,708
Physician G	5,880	8.87%	$135,000	$474,989	($214,286)	($88,700)	$307,003
	66,362	100.00%	$945,000	$5,355,000	($1,500,000)	($1,000,000)	$3,800,000
			15%	85%	60%	40%	

©2009 Coker Group

billing costs, etc., can indeed vary with productivity, but these variable costs typically represent a small portion of overall expenses. Accordingly, even when using RVUs to allocate expenses, at least 50% should be allocated equally with only the remaining costs being allocated based on productivity. Thus, a similar calculation occurs with overhead expenses, but a larger portion is shared equally. This concept is illustrated in Table 4-4.

In Table 4-4, the revenue totals $6,300,000 and expenses are $2,500,000; thus, the profit before physician expenses is still $3,800,000, similar to the example above. In this example, revenue will be allocated 15% equally and 85% based on wRVU productivity. Expenses will be allocated 60% equally and 40% based on wRVU productivity.

Revenue allocation for Physician A is calculated as follows:

Equal: $6,300,000 x 15% / 7 = $135,000
Productivity: $6,300,000 x 85% x 17.02% = $911,421
Total: $1,046,421

Physician A's expense allocation is calculated as follows:

Equal: $2,500,000 x 60% / 7 = $214,286
Productivity: $2,500,000 x 40% x 17.02% = $170,200
Total: $384,486

Based on the net of these two calculations, Physician A's profit before physician expenses totals $661,935.

Summary

There is a lot of flexibility in how wRVUs are used as an allocation method in private practice. Prior to implementing wRVUs as the productivity measure of choice, the practice should study the effects on the compensation plan and distribution process. Furthermore, there should be some additional analysis of the differences in productivity when comparing wRVUs, collections, and gross charges. In some cases, wRVUs may not be the best measure of productivity or they may need to be blended with one or more other productivity measures to create the most equitable allocation tool. In any case, wRVUs are a valuable measure and should always be considered as a potential method of allocation.

HOSPITAL-EMPLOYED SETTINGS

The use of wRVUs to compensate physicians is currently the norm within hospital-employed settings. While specific statistics surrounding their prevalence is unavailable, it would not be a stretch to estimate that 9 out of every 10 physician employment agreements are using wRVUs in some form as the productivity measure. There are many reasons for this, but one of the key reasons is that the hospital knows that it will be difficult to retain physicians if they pay them based only on the profits of their practice or on what the practice is able to collect. In most hospital settings, the payer mix is worse than in private practice and numerous inefficiencies exist wherein the practice does not generate enough profit before physician expenses to represent a market wage. Further, the lack of control is another significant factor, with the physician believing they can most impact their productivity, much more so that overhead structure, payer contracting, payer mix, and the efficiency of the billing office. As a result, many look outside the realm of practice profitability for a means of compensating physicians.

This concept of not compensating directly on practice profits is not new. Many historical contracts used gross charges as a compensation method. We've already explained the downfalls to this. As many hospitals around the country continue to ramp up their employment of physicians, the use of wRVUs is the chosen alternative.

RVUs are used in countless ways in physician employment contracts. We explain many of the conceptual uses below.

Basic wRVU Model

In the most basic wRVU model, a physician's accumulated wRVUs are multiplied by a conversion factor (compensation to wRVU ratio), which translates wRVUs into actual cash compensation. This basic model is illustrated in the following equation:

FIGURE 4.1 Basic RVU Model

The wRVUs "are what they are," but the conversion factor is established by the health system. A number of different factors go into establishing the rate per wRVU, not the least of which is fair market value and commercial reasonableness considerations. In general, the following factors should be considered:

- Historical compensation/productivity/financial data of the physician
- Coding audit results
- Payer mix and payer contracted rates
- Industry benchmark data
  - Medical Group Management Association (MGMA)
  - Sullivan, Cotter, and Associates (SCA)
  - American Medical Group Association (AMGA)
- Local market data (if available)
- Other components of the compensation model

Health systems often oversimplify the establishment of the conversion factor. Oftentimes this is a result of them applying the "pick a percentile" method, wherein they open up an industry survey, pick a percentile (oftentimes the median), and then apply this to the compensation model. The result is not always market-based compensation and many times can lead to overcompensating physicians. Thus, proper diligence should be applied in establishing the rate per wRVU.

Another common issue with conversion factors is that the employment agreement establishes a fixed conversion factor for a period of years and there is no flexibility for the hospital to update the conversion factor. Often, changes can occur in the hospital's specific financial situation or in the overall healthcare industry that warrant the conversion factors in a compensation model to be updated. This especially is the case in today's highly volatile healthcare industry wherein large reimbursement cuts could render the current conversion factors financially unviable. The opposite is true as well. If the conversion factors are not revisited regularly, recruitment/retention issues could arise if the rates slowly fall below market. Thus, conversion factors should be revisited annually and recalibrated as necessary. Caution should be heeded with respect to establishing a cost of living (COLA) adjustment to the conversion factor. Although this is easy, it does not necessarily make the conversion factor consistent with the market.

One final note with respect to establishing a conversion factor is the order of operations. Often, a health system will establish a base compensation for a physician, look up the associated productivity percentile for that level of base compensation in an industry survey, and use these two variables to derive a rate per wRVU. This assumes an appropriate correlation between compensation and productivity that is directly applicable to the respective market of the health system, which is likely not the case. Thus, it is best to establish base compensation, then establish the rate per wRVU (using the data outlined above), and then use these two variables to establish a wRVU threshold.

The basic wRVU model can be tailored in many ways. One of these is in relation to treatment of base compensation. Within a wRVU model, base compensation can be either completely risk-based, with no guaranteed compensation, or a reasonable level of guaranteed pay can be established in which productivity incentives become effective only when a certain threshold of productivity is achieved. If

TABLE 4-5 Basic wRVU Model with Guaranteed Compensation		
	Scenario One	**Scenario Two**
Base Compensation	$200,000	$200,000
wRVU Threshold	5,000	5,000
Conversion Factor	$40.00	$40.00
wRVUs Produced	5,500	4,500
wRVU Compensation	$20,000	$0
Total Compensation	**$220,000**	**$200,000**

©2009 Coker Group

guaranteed compensation will be provided, it is important not to set the guaranteed pay too high, as it will remove any incentives that are inherent to the model.

Table 4-5 is an example of this basic wRVU model where there is a guaranteed level of compensation. In this example, the guaranteed compensation is $200,000. Using a conversion factor of $40.00, this level of guaranteed pay is aligned with a productivity threshold of 5,000 wRVUs. Only when the physician achieves this level of productivity will there be a potential for additional incentive compensation.

In Scenario One, the physician exceeds the wRVU threshold and therefore generates an additional $20,000 of compensation. In Scenario Two, the wRVU threshold is not achieved and therefore only the base compensation is paid. Should the model be completely risk-based, Scenario Two would have resulted in $180,000 (4,500 x $40.00) of compensation to the physician.

Tiered wRVU Model

Another modification that can occur within a wRVU-based model is adding a "tiering" affect. Typically, the most basic wRVU model includes only one conversion factor; however, many models can become more complex by including one or more additional tiers such that as productivity increases, compensation increases at a slightly higher level. The premise behind this is that once fixed costs are covered (discussed above), additional income is available that can be shared with the physician, as only variable costs are then being incurred.

Table 4-6 illustrates a tiered wRVU model. In this case, the model includes two tiers. As productivity increases for the physician, a higher conversion factor results. At the start of the movement to wRVU-based models, many of the models were

TABLE 4-6 Tiered wRVU Model			
Tier	**Low End of Range**	**High End of Range**	**Conversion Factor**
One	–	5,000	$37.00
Two	5,000		$40.00

©2009 Coker Group

tiered. In many instances there were four or five tiers. After health systems grappled with the administrative challenges of administering such a complex model, the concept of tiering diminished somewhat in favor of less-complex models. Thus, if tiering does exist, it tends to only include two tiers, three at the most.

To illustrate exactly how this compensation model works, let's assume a physician generates 6,750 wRVUs. If this were the case, the calculation shown in Table 4.7 would result.

Thus, the physician's compensation per wRVU increases as productivity increases. There are benefits to this model in that there is added incentive to be more productive. In addition, it compensates those who are marginally productive at a lower conversion factor. In some respects, the perceived benefit is more psychological than economical. For example, in this example, if all wRVUs were paid at $37.00, total compensation would be $249,750. Thus, the impact of tiering creates only a $5,250 (2%) increase.

Using this same concept, some health systems have chosen to insert a penalty tier for those physicians who are not producing at an appropriate level. This only works if base compensation is a draw, as the guarantee would mitigate the impact of the penalty tier. As an example, a health system may expect a typical family practice physician to produce at least 4,000 wRVUs a year. The starting rate per is $40. Thus, if producing 4,000 wRVUs, compensation totals $1,600. However, if a physician is producing less than 4,000 wRVUs, the rate applied is muchlower, $33.00 per wRVU. Thus a physician generating 3,500 wRVUs would only be paid $115,500. The wRVU level is only 12.5% lower, but compensation is approximately 28% lower. This provides substantial incentive to at least meet the minimum production level, but also recognizes the impact that lower productivity levels have on physician practices as a result of most overhead being fixed.

Pay Band Model

The pay band model is another wRVU-based productivity model, but it is slightly different than the basic wRVU model. This model matches compensation percentiles to wRVU percentiles for each respective specialty using the most recent survey data, likely the MGMA. Similar to the heavily tiered wRVU model, due to the complexities of the pay band model, fewer health systems tend to use it, but it is still a viable model in many respects.

The calculation of compensation occurs on a quarterly basis wherein each physician's wRVU productivity level for the past 12 months is compared to industry benchmarks and the compensation is adjusted to this benchmark. For example, under the most basic scenario, if a physician is producing at the 45th percentile for the past 12 months, his compensation level is adjusted to be in line with the 45th compensation percentile and he is paid at this level for the next three months. At the end of the quarter, the past 12 months of wRVUs is once again compared to benchmark levels and is adjusted accordingly. For example, if productivity increased to the 55th percentile, compensation would follow and be paid at this level for the next three months. If productivity decreased to the 40th percentile, compensation would also decrease to this level for the next three months. Thus, this model is completely dependent on the physician's level of productivity.

TABLE 4-7   Example of Tiered wRVU Model

Tier	High End of Range	Conversion Factor	Compensation
One	5,000	$37.00	$185,000
Two	1,750	$40.00	$70,000
Total Compensation	6,750		$255,000

©2009 Coker Group

While the most basic pay band model perfectly aligns compensation and productivity, this does not have to be the case (and likely should not be the case in most instances). For example, a higher level of productivity could be required to achieve a certain level of compensation or vice versa. Thus, the model could be set to where median productivity results in 40th percentile compensation, or 40th percentile productivity results in median compensation. This can be compared to the most basic model wherein median productivity results in median compensation. Just as the conversion factor should be adjusted based on various local market factors, the alignment within this model should be adjusted considering the same factors. The one challenge in this instance is that if the alignment needs to be adjusted to where a higher level of productivity is required for a lower level of compensation (i.e., 50th percentile productivity = 40th percentile compensation), the overtness of this misalignment may be perceived negatively by the physicians. Thus, education and transparency are important as they relate to establishing the alignment between productivity and compensation in this model.

This model can also incorporate a guaranteed level of compensation; however, it must be low enough to allow the model to respond to changes in productivity. Thus, guaranteed compensation in this model is lower than that in the other wRVU model.

Table 4-8 provides an example of this model. We have used hypothetical wRVU data.

TABLE 4-8   Sample wRVU Productivity Data

	wRVUs	12 Month Rolling wRVUs
Q1- 2011	1,834	
Q2- 2011	1,886	
Q3- 2011	2,047	
Q4- 2011	1,843	7,610
Q1- 2012	2,156	7,932
Q2- 2012	1,737	7,783

©2009 Coker Group

TABLE 4-9 Sample Pay Band Compensation for Three Quarters	
Beginning of Q1- 2012	
Past 12 Month wRVUs	7,610
wRVU %tile	59th
Compensation %tile	59th
Annual Compensation	$343,330
Quarterly Compensation	$85,833
Beginning of Q2- 2012	
Past 12 Month wRVUs	7,932
wRVU %tile	63rd
Compensation %tile	63rd
Annual Compensation	$357,830
Quarterly Compensation	$89,458
Beginning of Q3- 2012	
Past 12 Month wRVUs	7,783
wRVU %tile	61st
Compensation %tile	61st
Annual Compensation	$351,286
Quarterly Compensation	$87,822

©2009 Coker Group

Table 4-9 illustrates the pay band compensation calculation for three quarters. Per this example, the physician's productivity is in line with the 59th percentile for the 12 months ending just prior to Q1- 2012. Thus, for Q1- 2012 he is compensated at the 59th percentile. At the end of Q1- 2012, the physician's productivity has increased to the 63rd percentile; thus, for Q2- 2012, he is compensated at this higher percentile. In Q2- 2012, productivity decreases slightly; thus, a lower percentile of compensation is paid in Q3- 2012.

Incentives for Shift-Based Physicians

Another method of using wRVUs to compensate physicians is geared to physicians who primarily work shifts, such as hospitalists. In such a model, the physicians are usually paid a guaranteed wage per shift and there is very little incentive included. Thus, a wRVU threshold will be established for each shift. As an example, for a hospitalist, the threshold could be 30 wRVUs per daytime shift and 15 wRVUs per nighttime shift. Should the physician exceed this level of wRVUs, then additional compensation will be provided for all incremental wRVUs at a pre-established conversion factor.

In these types of scenarios, a study must determine what the typical wRVU productivity is on a given shift so as to establish the appropriate threshold. To set it too low would result in the physician receiving additional compensation for the "normal" amount of work performed wherein the incentive is really geared toward compensating the physician for performing extra work.

CONCLUSION

In this chapter, we explained the basic uses of wRVUs for compensating physicians in both private practice and hospital-employed settings. The examples form the foundation of the majority of models that exist. Using these basic premises, an infinite amount of customization can occur so the model will meet the specific needs of the practice. For example, the guaranteed compensation can be increased or completely removed, the conversion factor can be increased or decreased, some pooling of wRVUs can occur to provide group incentives, and so on. The number of possibilities with these models is truly endless.

It is important to once again emphasize, though, that wRVUs are not necessarily directly correlated with actual practice performance. A physician can generate a substantial number of wRVUs but, due to payer mix issues, billing office inefficiencies, etc., the wRVUs could not translate into actual dollars. Thus, caution must be taken to be prudent in establishing the parameters of the model and reviewing them regularly to ensure the overall structure makes sense and represents a mutually beneficial relationship between the physician and the practice/hospital.

RVU Compensation —Legal Aspects

This chapter provides an overview of the legal aspects of RVU-based physician compensation systems. As is described elsewhere in this book, physician compensation structures include compensation that may be determined based on many things, including gross revenue, net collections, RVUs, tiered RVUs, bonuses, and other systems of allocation. Most compensation systems involve one part of the physician compensation that is typically fixed-base salary and an additional component that is a bonus.

THE LEGAL BASIS FOR RVUS

RVUs are established by CMS in the Code of Federal Regulations (CFR) at 42 CFR 414.22. These sections of the CFR describe in detail how to calculate RVUs.

RVU-based compensation is recognized in the Stark Law where productivity bonuses based on RVUs are approved as an appropriate and lawful method to compensate physicians. See 42 CFR 411.352(i)(3)(i) "Special Rule for productivity bonuses and profit shares." This exception allows the payment of productivity bonuses based on services performed personally by the physician or an immediate family member of the physician.

A number of other legal considerations are associated with RVU-compensation systems as follows: federal Stark Law, federal Anti-Kickback law, federal Advisory Opinions from the Office of the Inspector General, federal tax law, state Anti-Kickback statutes, state corporate practice of medicine statutes, the Federal False Claims Act, and the Medicare prohibition against assignment of receivables, among others. Each of these areas of law can have an impact on RVU-based physician compensation. Please note that the Medicaid system provides no guidance in this regard and appears to rely on Medicare.

THE STARK LAW

Regardless of the special rule for productivity bonuses described above, the base salary and other elements of physician compensation systems must meet other legal requirements. The Stark Law is the most restrictive and also the most punitive of all of these laws. If the requirements of the Stark Law are met or one of its exceptions are met, then in many cases the requirements of the other laws mentioned above also will be met.

The Stark Law prohibits a physician from making a referral of a designated health service if the physician has a direct or indirect financial relationship with the entity unless a specific exception applies. Each of the exceptions is very specifically worded and must be strictly complied with. If strict compliance with these exceptions is not achieved, the violation may carry with it substantial fines and penalties, including, in serious cases, exclusion from the Medicare program.

Even practitioners who do not have the majority of their practice within the Medicare system must comply with the Stark Law if they participate in Medicare. Those elements of the physician's practice that are outside of Medicare, or are not involved in designated health service, are technically not covered by the Stark Law, but it is rare to find an organization that will keep two separate billing systems and two separate recordkeeping systems, with one for complying with Stark and one for a different compensation system that is not Stark-compliant. As a result, virtually every physician compensation arrangement comes within the coverage of the Stark Law for practical reasons or for legal reasons.

The fines and penalties under the Stark Law are severe. These are civil penalties that typically would not involve imprisonment, but the fines can be large; for example, fines of up to $15,000 per claim are permissible. It doesn't matter if the claim was for $1 or 10 cents, there could be a fine of $15,000 per claim. When those $15,000 fines are multiplied by the thousands of claims made by a physician, the fines can become astronomical, amounting to tens or hundreds of millions of dollars in cases where the reimbursements obtained are comparatively small.

Other fines and penalties can be imposed under the other laws mentioned above, but the ultimate penalty is exclusion from the Medicare program. Few medical practitioners, hospitals, or facilities can survive without participation in the Medicare program.

EXCEPTIONS TO THE STARK LAW

Although the Stark Law has a very broad application to designated health services, including in most cases any form of physician compensation utilizing RVU systems, productivity bonuses utilizing an RVU system are a lawfully recognized exception under Stark.

Additionally, there are two principal exceptions for general compensation systems: 1) the bona fide employment exception for W-2 employees and 2) the personal services arrangement exception for independent contractors.

To understand how the exceptions work, it is necessary to start with definitions under the Stark Law. The definitions are some of the most critical terms included in this regulatory regime.

1. *Physician.* The definition of physician is surprisingly broad. It includes a variety of practitioners, including doctors of medicine, osteopathy, dentists, podiatrists, optometrists, and chiropractors. It also includes immediate family

members of physicians, such as husbands and wives, parents, children, and siblings, as well as more distant relations such as stepparents, stepchildren, stepsiblings, in-laws, grandparents, grandchildren, and their spouses.

2. *Designated Health Services.* The definition of Designated Health Services (DHS) is crucial to understanding how the Stark Law works. The DHS list is annually updated and published in the Federal Register using CPT codes to more precisely define these terms. The DHS list is as follows:

   a. Clinical laboratory services;
   b. Physical therapy services;
   c. Occupational therapy services;
   d. Radiology services including MRI, CT, and ultrasound;
   e. Radiation therapy services and supplies;
   f. Durable medical equipment and supplies;
   g. Parenteral and enteral nutrients, equipment and supplies;
   h. Prosthetics, orthotics, prosthetic devices, and supplies;
   i. Home health services;
   j. Outpatient prescription drugs; and
   k. Inpatient and outpatient hospital services.

You can see that outpatient medical care in a physician's office is not on the list. Additionally, it is notable that surgery is not DHS under Stark.

To the extent that physician compensation in a medical group does not involve anything that is on the DHS list, that compensation is free of the restrictions that are in the Stark Law. However, all physicians who are employed by hospitals are covered by Stark because that is on the DHS list as "inpatient and outpatient hospital services." Additionally, the referral of a DHS item by a physician in a medical group is covered by Stark and that list is extensive. As a result of the pervasive coverage of the DHS list, most medical groups structure their compensation arrangements in strict compliance with Stark.

Any direct or indirect compensation arrangement or ownership or investment, or any arrangement involving payment to a physician by an entity, is considered a compensation arrangement under Stark if DHS is involved in or referred by the practice. This covers salary, bonuses, income guarantees, medical director payments, and on-call fees, in any form including RVUs.

STARK EXCEPTION FOR BONA FIDE EMPLOYMENT RELATIONSHIPS

The Stark Law does provide an exception for bona fide employment relationships. These cover any amount paid by an employer to a physician (or an immediate family member of such physician) who has a bona fide employment relationship with the employer for the provision of services if:

1. The employment is for identifiable services.
2. The amount of the compensation:

     a. Is consistent with the fair market value of the services; and

     b. Is not determined in a manner that takes into account (directly or indirectly) the volume or value of any referrals by the referring physician.

3. The compensation is provided pursuant to an agreement that would be commercially reasonable even if no referrals were made to the employer.

STARK EXCEPTION FOR PERSONAL SERVICE ARRANGEMENTS

A Stark exception also exists for personal service arrangements for situations that involve someone who is not a W-2 employee if:

1. The arrangement is set out in writing, signed by the parties, and specifies the services covered by the arrangement;

2. The arrangement covers all of the services to be provided to the entity by the physician (or an immediate family member of such physician);

3. The aggregate services contracted for do not exceed those that are reasonable and necessary for the legitimate business purposes of the arrangement;

4. The term of the arrangement is for at least one year;

5. The compensation to be paid over the term of the arrangement is set in advance, does not exceed fair market value, and is not determined in a manner that takes into account the volume or value of any referrals or other business generated between the parties; and

6. The services to be performed under the arrangement do not involve the counseling or promotion or a business arrangement or other activity that violates any state or federal law.

STARK DEFINITION FOR FAIR MARKET VALUE

The definition of fair market value is very important under Stark. The term "fair market value" means the value in arm's-length transactions, consistent with the general market value. "General market value" means the price that an asset would bring as the result of bona fide bargaining between well-informed buyers and sellers who are not otherwise in a position to generate business for the other party, or the compensation that would be included in a service agreement as the result of bona fide bargaining between well-informed parties to the agreement who are not otherwise in a position to generate business for the other party at the time of the service agreement.

    Usually, the fair market price is the compensation that has been included in bona fide service agreements with comparable terms at the time of the agreement, where the compensation has not been determined in any manner that takes into account the volume or value of anticipated or actual referrals.

SPECIAL RULE FOR PRODUCTIVITY BONUSES AND PROFIT SHARES IN GROUP PRACTICES

A physician in a group practice may be paid a share of "overall profits" of the group, provided that the share is not determined in any manner that is directly related to the volume or value of referrals of DHS by the physician.

Additionally, a physician in the group practice may be paid a productivity bonus based on services that he or she has personally performed, or services "incident to" such personally performed services, or both, provided that the bonus is not determined in any manner that is directly related to the volume or value of referrals of DHS by the physician.

"Overall profits" means the group's entire profits derived from DHS payable by Medicare or Medicaid or the profits derived from DHS payable by Medicare or Medicaid of any component of the group practice that consists of at least five physicians.

Overall profits should be divided in a reasonable and verifiable manner that is not directly related to the volume or value of the physician's referrals of DHS. The share of overall profits will be deemed not to relate directly to the volume or value of referrals if one of the following conditions is met:

1. The group's profits are divided per capita (for example, per member of the group or per physician in the group); or
2. Revenues derived from DHS are distributed based on the distribution of the group practice's revenues attributed to services that are not DHS payable by any federal healthcare program or private payer; or
3. Revenues derived from DHS constitute less than 5% of the group practice's total revenues, and the allocated portion of those revenues to each physician in the group practice constitutes 5% or less of his or her total compensation from the group.

A *productivity bonus* must be calculated in a reasonable and verifiable manner that is not directly related to the volume or value of the physician's referrals of DHS. A productivity bonus will be deemed not to relate directly to the volume or value of referrals of DHS if one of the following conditions is met:

1. The bonus is based on the physician's total patient encounters or relative value units (RVUs);
2. The bonus is based on the allocation of the physician's compensation attributable to services that are not DHS payable by an federal health care program or private payer; and
3. Another exception exists if revenues derived from DHS are less than 5% of the group practice's total revenues, and the allocated portion of those revenues to each physician in the group practice constitutes 5% or less of his or her total compensation from the group practice.

Every medical group must maintain thorough documentation of the systems, calculations, and processes that are used to determine physician compensation.

SPECIAL RULES ON COMPENSATION

The following special rules apply:

1. Compensation is considered "set in advance" if the aggregate compensation, a time-based or per-unit of service-based (whether per-use or per-service) amount, or a specific formula for calculating the compensation, is set in an agreement between the parties before the furnishing of the items or services for which the compensation is to be paid. The formula for determining the compensation must be set forth in sufficient detail so that it can be objectively verified, and the formula may not be changed or modified during the course of the agreement in any manner that takes into account the volume or value of referrals or other business generated by the referring physician.

2. Unit-based compensation (including time-based or per-unit of service-based compensation) is deemed not to take into account "the volume or value of referrals" if the compensation is fair market value for services or items actually provided and does not vary during the course of the compensation arrangement in any manner that takes into account referrals of DHS.

3. Unit-based compensation (including time-based or per-unit of service-based compensation) is deemed not to take into account "other business generated between the parties," provided that the compensation is fair market value for items and services actually provided and does not vary during the course of the compensation arrangement in any manner that takes into account referrals or other business generated by the referring physician, including private pay healthcare business (except for services personally performed by the referring physician, which are not considered "other business generated" by the referring physician).

LIMITING REFERRALS

A physician's compensation from a bona fide employer or under a managed care contract or other contract for personal services may be conditioned on the physician's referrals to a particular provider, practitioner, or supplier, as long as the compensation arrangement meets all of the following conditions:

1. Is set in advance for the term of the agreement;
2. Is consistent with fair market value for services performed and the payment does not take into account the volume or value of anticipated or required referrals; and
3. Complies with both of the following conditions:
   a. The requirement to make referrals to a particular provider, practitioner, or supplier is set forth in a written agreement signed by the parties; and
   b. The requirement to make referrals to a particular provider, practitioner, or supplier does not apply if the patient expresses a preference for a different provider, practitioner, or supplier; the patient's insurer deter-

mines the provider, practitioner, or supplier; or the referral is not in the patient's best medical interests in the physician's judgment.

4. The required referrals relate solely to the physician's services covered by the scope of the employment or the contract, and the referral requirement is reasonably necessary to effectuate the legitimate business purposes of the compensation arrangement. In no event may the physician be required to make referrals that relate to services that are not provided by the physician under the scope of his or her employment or contract.

DEFINITION OF GROUP PRACTICE

The rules above on the allocation of overall profits and productivity bonuses are available to group practices. The term "group practice" means a group of two or more physicians legally organized as a partnership, professional corporation, foundation, not-for-profit corporation, faculty practice plan, or similar association:

1. In which each physician who is a member of the group provides substantially the full range of services which the physician routinely provides, including medical care, consultation, diagnosis, or treatment, through the joint use of shared office space, facilities, equipment and personnel;

2. For which substantially all of the services of the physicians who are members of the group are provided through the group and are billed under a billing number assigned to the group and amounts so received are treated as receipts of the group;

3. In which the overhead expenses of and the income from the practice are distributed in accordance with methods previously determined;

4. Except as provided in subparagraph (B)(i), of the Stark Law in which no physician who is a member of the group directly or indirectly receives compensation based on the volume or value of referrals by the physician;

5. In which members of the group personally conduct no less than 75% of the physician-patient encounters of the group practice; and

6. Which meets such other standards as the U.S. Secretary of Health and Human Services may impose by regulation.

THE ANTI-KICKBACK STATUTE (AKS)

The anti-kickback statute prohibits knowing or willful payments of any kind of inducement in return for referrals. Therefore, to avoid being attacked for a violation of the anti-kickback statute, it is necessary to make sure that payments are not made with the intent to induce referrals and also not made with the intent to limit medically necessary services for patients. Thankfully, safe harbors are available.

The terms of the safe harbor most often used is generally known as the "personal services and the management contracts" safe harbor. This requires that the physician compensation agreement meet seven standards: 1) the agreement must be in writing; 2) the agreement must describe all of the services to be provided; 3) if the agreement is periodic, sporadic, or part-time, it must specify exactly the schedule of the intervals; 4) the agreement must be for no less than one year; 5) compensation must be set in advance, consistent with fair market value, and not determined in a manner that takes into account the volume or value of referrals, 6) it cannot involve the counseling or promotion of a business that violates state or federal law; and 7) the aggregate services do not exceed those reasonable necessary to accomplish the commercially reasonable purposes of the agreement.

When parties enter these agreements, determining what is set in advance, fair market value, and commercially reasonable are the most difficult aspects of the agreements. Typically, it is necessary to engage a third-party valuation organization to review and comment on the terms of the compensation agreements to assure that the agreement is properly set in advance, fair market value, and commercially reasonable.

Generally, if the Stark exceptions are met, the compensation arrangement will also meet the anti-kickback safe harbor.

NOT-FOR-PROFIT TAX RULES

If a not-for-profit hospital is the employer, additional rules apply. It is illegal to allow "tax exempt" dollars to be paid to "taxable" individual physicians unless the payment is justified by the delivery of services of equal value. Those services may be compensated only at fair market value. In these situations, fair market value should be determined by an independent third party or by comparison to an independent compensation survey. If private inurement or private benefit occurs, the hospital's tax except status could be lost. Once an RVU compensation system is established, the RVU structure must be reviewed by an independent third-party valuation consultant. Or, at the very least, it must be compared to a valuation survey to verify that the RVU system results in overall compensation that is competitive and within the ranges of compensation that is paid to other similar practitioners.

CREDENTIALING

Economic credentialing systems also can be linked to RVU compensation systems. Hospitals use economic credentialing to do physician profiling and loyalty determinations. To the extent that a physician scores poorly in his or her RVU compensation, a hospital that does economic credentialing can use the RVU statistics against a practitioner.

Economic credentialing frequently has been challenged in lawsuits. However, hospitals have successfully justified the practice in most cases in those states when the matter is not prevented by law.

SUMMARY

RVU compensation systems are a recognized lawful system for productivity bonuses. However, other legal requirements must be met to assure that overall compensation is appropriately paid. It is best to make sure that compensation is fair market value, commercially reasonable, and set in advance in a written agreement of one year or more.

RVUs and Productivity

RVUs clearly are the key measure of physician productivity in the healthcare industry. In previous chapters we discussed many of the reasons for this; thus, there is no need for an in-depth review in this chapter. However, to provide a brief overview, gross charges are no longer used due to the variability in establishing physician fee schedules and their dramatic influence on productivity. Collections are of utmost importance in private practice and are still primarily used to determine physician compensation in this environment, but they also are an imperfect measure of true productivity because of the various factors influencing collections. These factors include, but are not limited to, payer mix, ability to negotiate favorable managed-care contracts, revenue cycle management, and geographical location.

There are other types of more "pure" productivity measures, but even these are rarely used. For example, patient volume can be an illustration of productivity. Patient volume is not affected by many of the factors that impact collections. For example, the type of payer does not have any influence on the figure nor does geographical location of a physician. However, one must define patient volume and consistently report it in order for it to be a good productivity measure.

Some could define patient volume as all patient encounters, including office visits and surgery. If a physician sees a patient in the office and then performs a surgical procedure, does this count as two in terms of patient volume or just one? To be useful, the entire industry must report this measure in a similar fashion.

The issues with the above productivity measures once again lead to the use of RVUs. This is because of their objectivity and ability to be universally applied in a similar manner. For example, a physician in Washington, Indiana, will report RVUs in a similar manner to a physician in Seattle, Washington. Because CMS establishes the metrics, there is minimal influence on behalf of a physician. Two physicians in the same specialty and same city who charge the same mix of CPT codes over the period of a year could have very different gross charges and collections, but their RVUs should be identical. This is the beauty of RVUs. Of course, the debate about RVUs is whether the values assigned to each CPT code are correct. Although each physician throughout the industry could take issue with certain codes, overall, the RVUs established for each CPT code are widely accepted.

Similar to compensation, work relative value units (wRVUs) are used primarily in evaluating physician productivity, while practice expense RVUs can be used to further evaluate the performance of a medical practice. The use of practice expense RVUs is explored in later chapters, thus the focus in this chapter is the use of wRVUs in evaluating a physician's productivity.

GETTING THE DATA

To evaluate productivity using wRVUs, the data must be available. wRVUs can be derived regardless of the complexity or age of a medical practice's practice management system. In many instances this can be as simple as running a system-generated report that already includes wRVU data. This clearly is the best alternative and provides for the most ease of use in terms of using wRVUs to measure productivity. Such reports are available only when RVU data has been previously loaded into the system's databases. For example, just as a practice loads in its fee schedule, it also loads in the Medicare Physician Fee Schedule, which includes not only overall reimbursement data for each CPT code, but also the associated RVUs. As medical practices continue to update their practice management systems and look to implementing electronic health records, RVU data is becoming more readily available as the newer systems are configured to allow reporting of these data.

One key consideration that is often overlooked is the need to update the RVU data in the system's databases on a regular basis. If the system is reporting wRVUs based on the 2006 Medicare Physician Fee Schedule for work performed in 2009, the wRVU data reported by the system will not be useful. This is because the RVU data are updated on a regular basis, as discussed in previous chapters. We recommend medical practices update the RVU data each January. However, if the medical practice is on a fiscal year that is not aligned with the calendar year, it may choose an alternative date in the year to update the RVU data in the system.

Even if a practice is still using an old practice management system that does not have the capability of reporting wRVUs directly from the system, wRVU data can still be obtained, albeit with more time and effort. Regardless of the age of the system, most are able to report CPT code data by physician. When this is the case, calculating wRVUs requires these data to be exported to a spreadsheet application, such as Microsoft Excel. If this can be done electronically, it is much preferred from a time perspective; however, many times the data can only be printed and then manually entered into the spreadsheet. Essentially, the only data needed are the physician, CPT code, and volume for the period under review.

To manually calculate wRVUs, the Medicare Physician Fee Schedule also must be available. This information can be obtained as a Microsoft Excel spreadsheet at no cost on Medicare's website (www.cms.gov). We recommend this information be saved on the user's computer so it is easily accessible. Once the CPT code data is in the spreadsheet and the Medicare Physician Fee Schedule is available, a simple formula can be written in Microsoft Excel to electronically match the wRVU value for each CPT code to the CPT code data for the physician. This formula is called a "vlookup" formula, which stands for "vertical lookup," one of Microsoft Excel's lookup and reference formulas. Essentially, this formula will look up a piece of data in the user's spreadsheet, which in this instance is the CPT code. The formula then matches the look-up value (the CPT code) with another set of data, in this instance the Medicare Physician Fee Schedule, and returns a value corresponding to the look-up value in the other set of data. Four inputs are required to complete this formula:

1. ***Look-Up Value:*** This will be the CPT code. Thus, if the CPT code data are in column B, row 4, you would select this cell for use in the formula.
2. ***Table Array:*** This will be the Medicare Physician Fee Schedule. The table should start with the column where the CPT code is located in the Medicare Physician Fee Schedule and extend over to the wRVU data. If the Medicare Physician Fee Schedule is not modified from its original format, this would include columns A through F.
3. ***Column Index Number:*** This refers to the location of the data that is to be returned: the wRVU data. The value is entered in a numerical format, referencing the column number in the Medicare Physician Fee Schedule where the wRVU data is located. The columns should begin being counted where the look-up value is located in the Medicare Physician Fee Schedule. In the unmodified Medicare Physician Fee Schedule, the CPT code data is in column A and the wRVU data is in column F. With column A being considered "1," column B considered "2," etc., column F would be "6." As the wRVU data is six columns away from the CPT code data, "6" would be entered for this input.
4. ***Range Lookup:*** This refers to whether the formula should focus only on exact matches or the closest match. If "False" is entered, it will focus only on exact matches, and if "True" is entered, the formula will report the closest match to the CPT code being looked up. As we are dealing with very specific CPT codes, we only want an exact match; thus, "False" should always be entered in this input.

An example of the completed formula is outlined below. Note that, similar to other formulas, the various inputs are separated by commas.

=VLOOKUP(A2,'[Medicare Physician Fee Schedule 2013.xls] PPRRVU13'!$A:$F,6,FALSE)

In the above example, A2 is the Look-Up Value where the CPT code we are looking up is located; the next value, '[Medicare Physician Fee Schedule 2013.xls] PPRRVU13'!$A:$F, is the Table Array where the data we are looking up is located. The CPT code is located in column A; thus, the table starts with this column. The wRVU data being returned are in column F, so we are ending our table with this column. The next input of "6" recognizes that the data we want returned are six columns from the beginning of the table. And the last input is "False" as we only want exact matches to be returned.

The above formula, although seemingly somewhat complex, becomes second nature when used frequently. Furthermore, the formula has to be written only once and then can be copied for all other CPT codes that need a corresponding wRVU value. Thus, essentially it can be entered for the first CPT code being looked up and then "dragged down" for all of the following CPT codes that are being looked up.

Once the spreadsheet has the wRVU value for each CPT code, then the volume data must be multiplied by the wRVU data to derive the total number of wRVUs for that CPT code. Then, the wRVUs for each CPT code can be added together to derive the total wRVUs for that physician. Table 6-1 is an example of what the end result (data worksheet) would look like.

Clearly, the manual tabulation of wRVUs can appear daunting, but it can be accomplished in a limited amount of time. This is especially the case when CPT code data can be exported directly from a practice management system into a spreadsheet. If the data have to be entered manually, this is the most time- consuming portion of the process. Once the data is in the system, the above formula and other calculations can be accomplished in approximately 5 to 10 minutes per physician. Considering that this will be done no more than monthly, this is reasonable and worthwhile to have a superior productivity measure.

ADJUSTMENTS TO WORK RVUS

By and large, the wRVU data manually tabulated or generated by a system report do not need any further adjustment and can be analyzed as is. With this being said, certain factors should be considered that may warrant adjusting. These are mainly situations where the wRVU credit may need to be discounted to be in line with the reimbursement received. There are two situations where this primarily occurs: surgical assistance and performing multiple procedures.

TABLE 6-1   Data Worksheet Example

CPT Code	Volume	wRVU Values	wRVUs
10021	4	1.27	5.08
10060	4	1.22	4.88
10061	2	2.45	4.90
43280	4	18.10	72.40
43450	1	1.38	1.38
43520	1	11.29	11.29
43640	1	19.56	19.56
44005	8	18.46	147.68
99212	37	0.48	17.76
99213	195	0.97	189.15
99214	87	1.50	130.50
99215	7	2.11	14.77
99217	3	1.28	3.84

©2013 Coker Group

When a physician performs multiple procedures on the same patient during the same session (identified with modifier 51), it results in a reduction in reimbursement for all but the highest-ranked procedure. In calculating wRVUs, this should be considered if it is a prevalent issue, as a physician could be given full wRVU credit for the multiple procedures when only partial reimbursement was received for them. This could potentially skew any productivity comparisons and possibly result in overcompensation if wRVUs are being used as a compensation mechanism. Thus, the wRVU credit for multiple procedures can be discounted in line with the reimbursement trend or via some other fashion.

A similar issue occurs when a physician assists another physician in performing a surgical procedure (identified with modifiers 80, 81, or 82). While the physician who is actually performing the procedure gets to bill for the full amount, the surgeon acting in an assistant role does not get to bill for the full amount—only 20% of the allowable amount. Once again, if this is a prevalent service a physician provides, providing full wRVU credit will skew productivity. Thus, it is necessary to reduce the wRVU credit provided by some amount. This should most likely be aligned with the 20% that is allowable for reimbursement.

BENCHMARKING WORK RVUS

There is much more complexity in obtaining the wRVU data than there is in analyzing the data. Once again, if the practice management system can automatically generate this data, even the data-gathering process is not an issue. There are several ways to analyze a physician's wRVUs, which are outlined below.

- Internal comparisons to other physicians in a similar specialty
- External comparisons to industry benchmarks
- Ratio analysis using compensation
- Ratio analysis using collections

We discuss all of the various analysis methods herein, but the most prevalent is external comparisons to industry benchmarks. This is because external sources contain the largest repository of data against which to benchmark performance.

Internal comparison of wRVUs is simplistic in that it involves merely comparing wRVUs from one physician to the next. Table 6-2 illustrates some of the same data featured in Chapter 4 when looking at compensation.

The data below are representative of cardiologists within the same practice. Physicians A through F are all interventional cardiologists; Physician G is a noninvasive cardiologist. In comparing these physicians, we can note that there is some variance in productivity, with Physician A being the highest producer and Physician D being the lowest producer of the interventional cardiologists. Specifically, the highest producer is 40% more productive than the lowest producer. Four of the six interventional cardiologists have similar productivity levels.

Essentially, this is the type of internal analysis data that is possible. When performing such, it is important to remember the qualitative aspects of the practice. To use the example above, are their certain tasks Drs. C and D are completing that

TABLE 6-2   Internal Comparisons for Compensation Example

Physician		wRVUs
Physician A	11,297	17.02%
Physician B	10,739	16.18%
Physician C	9,091	13.70%
Physician D	8,124	12.24%
Physician E	10,428	15.71%
Physician F	10,803	16.28%
Physician G	5,880	8.87%
	66,362	100.00%

©2013 Coker Group

do not carry many wRVUs, but are critical to the overall success of the practice? If so, they should not be held to the same standard as the others. Also, the analysis can extend much more beyond an annual comparison. Depending on the availability of the data, it would be beneficial to obtain them on a monthly or quarterly basis and perform some trending analyses using graphs and other tools that better allow visualization of the data. Figure 6-1 is an example of the above data, charted on a quarterly basis.

Comparing data to external benchmarks uses the same data that are pulled for internal comparison purposes. This can also be done on a monthly, quarterly, or annual basis. Most, if not all, of the industry benchmarking data are reported on an annual basis; thus some conversion must occur to allow for monthly or quarterly comparisons. This can be done easily by annualizing the actual data or dividing the benchmark data by 12 to allow for a monthly comparison, or by 4 to allow for a quarterly comparison.

There are numerous sources of industry-benchmark wRVU data. Below are several sources that include wRVU data that are used most prevalently throughout the industry.

- Medical Group Management Association Physician Compensation and Production Survey (http://www.mgma.com/pm/article.aspx?id=28798)
- Medical Group Management Association Academic Practice Compensation and Production Survey (http://www.mgma.com/pm/article.aspx?id=28988)
- Sullivan, Cotter and Associates Physician Compensation and Productivity Survey (http://www.sullivancotter.com/surveys/index.php)
- American Medical Group Association Compensation and Financial Survey (https://ecommerce.amga.org/iMISpublic/Core/Orders/category.aspx?catid=3)

©2013 Coker Group

wRVUs

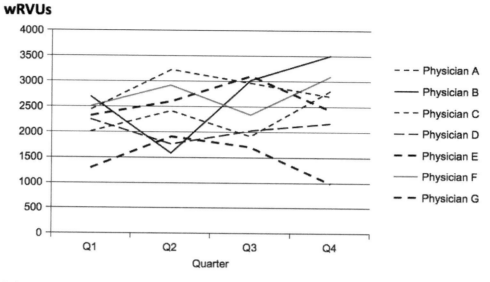

FIGURE 6-1   Data Charted on Quarterly Basis Example
©2013 Coker Group

Of the above listings, the Medical Group Management Association (MGMA) Physician Compensation and Production Survey appears to be the most widely used. This is likely because of the MGMA name attached to it as well as the breadth of information and number of respondents. Of all the surveys, the MGMA survey provides the most detailed amount of data. For example, when there are enough respondents to allow for such, the MGMA survey can break the data down geographically, demographically, by hospital ownership, size of practice, etc. Furthermore, it shows all of the percentiles of data points as opposed to only the quartiles. For example, for a family practice physician who is producing 5,000 wRVUs, using the MGMA survey we can say the production is at the 54th percentile. Using other survey data, we would be able to say only that the physician is between the median and 75th percentile. Thus, the MGMA survey allows for much more detail comparisons, which is useful. The following example is the most basic wRVU data for the specialty of family practice from the MGMA survey.

Specialty	Providers	Practices	Mean	Std. Dev.	25th Percentile	Median	75th Percentile	90th Percentile
Family Practice (without OB)	4,886	590	4,946	1,791	3,832	4,815	5,897	7,082

The following is the most basic wRVU data for the specialty of family practice from the Sullivan, Cotter and Associates (SCA) survey.

Organization Type/Region	Specialty	Position Level	N	10th Percentile	25th Percentile	Mean	Median	75th Percentile	90th Percentile
National	Family Practice	Staff Physician	2,573	3,349	4,071	4,998	4,849	5,708	6,708

In comparing to benchmarks, two approaches are typically most useful. These are outlined below.

- Comparing directly to a specific percentile
- Calculating as a percentage of the median

Comparing wRVU productivity to a specific benchmark percentile is the most common method. Because the only source of data that provides information for each percentile is the MGMA, when comparing to other sources, the physician must be classified within the available categories; for example, "between the median and 75th percentile" or "slightly below the median." This indicates the value of the MGMA data as it is a much more concrete comparison to be able to state a specific percentile of productivity. For the physicians above, we have benchmarked their wRVUs using the MGMA Physician Compensation and Production Survey: 2012 Report Based on 2011 Data and the SCA 2012 Physician Compensation and Productivity Survey (Table 6-3). We have used the specialty of Cardiology: Interventional-Invasive. We did not benchmark Dr. G as this physician represented a different specialty.

Reviewing the data below, note how much more meaningful the MGMA data are than the SCA data due to the ability to clearly present the productivity level of the physician. It is our hope that in the future more benchmarking surveys will be provided in this level of detail. Another important point is the level of disparity in production levels the two surveys indicate. For example, Dr. C's wRVUs are at the 45th percentile of MGMA benchmarks, but slightly above the median of SCA benchmarks. Oftentimes, this can be due to the number of respondents for a particular specialty and data point. For example, the MGMA survey had 528 respondents for this data point, while the SCA survey had only 227. In most cases, the survey with the higher number of respondents is the best choice as it represents a larger mix of the physicians in the market, which should provide for more accurate data.

As noted below, the wRVU data can also be compared to the median. This method can be applied consistently across surveys, as all of them tend to provide

| TABLE 6-3 | Detail of MGMA Survey Data Sample | | |
Physician	wRVUs	MGMA	SCA
Physician A	11,297	70th %tile	Slightly below the 75th %tile (11,510)
Physician B	10,739	66th %tile	Between median (8,833) and 75th %tile (11,510)
Physician C	9,091	45th %tile	Slightly above median (8,833)
Physician D	8,124	34th %tile	Slightly below median (8,833)
Physician E	10,428	62nd %tile	Between median (8,833) and 75th %tile (11,510)
Physician F	10,803	67th %tile	Between median (8,833) and 75th %tile (11,510)

TABLE 6-4	Productivity Comparison Using MGMA and SCA Surveys		
Physician	**wRVUs**	**MGMA**	**SCA**
Physician A	11,297	120.10%	127.90%
Physician B	10,739	114.17%	121.58%
Physician C	9,091	96.65%	102.92%
Physician D	8,124	86.37%	91.97%
Physician E	10,428	110.86%	118.06%
Physician F	10,803	114.85%	122.30%

©2013 Coker Group

the median benchmark. Table 6-4 illustrates this type of productivity comparison using data from both the MGMA and SCA surveys. The median from the MGMA survey is 9,406, while the median from the SCA survey is 8,833.

The information provided from this comparison is useful on a stand-alone basis in gaining a perspective on a physician's productivity in relation to the midpoint for that specialty, but it also is very useful when considering other benchmarks alongside productivity.

An example of this is consideration of productivity and compensation. Just as productivity is compared to the median, compensation can be compared in a similar fashion. Then, the two can be compared to each other. This is useful when dealing with benchmark data that are not on a percentile basis. For example, with the MGMA survey, you could easily indicate that a physician is producing wRVUs at the 70th percentile and being compensated at the 64th percentile. This level of accuracy is not possible in the SCA survey and others. Thus, using a comparison in relation to the median allows for somewhat better comparability. For example, a user can note that a physician is producing at 150% of the median, but only being compensated at 115% of the median. In normal circumstances, one would expect the productivity and compensation as a percentage of the median to be correlated.

Using wRVUs as a form of productivity measure also can be useful in performing ratio analyses. The most common ratio calculated using wRVUs is a compensation to wRVU ratio (also known as a conversion factor). Essentially, this is calculated by dividing compensation by wRVUs for the same time period. In most cases, depending on the specialty, the conversion factor will range from $25 to $75, with the majority ranging from $37.50 to $52.50. Table 6-5 shows an example of the conversion factors calculated using the same data as presented above.

In this situation, as all of the physicians are in the same practice, they have similar conversion factors. This is because the income distribution plan they use is largely productivity-based, using wRVUs as the productivity metric. In other situations, even within the same specialty in the same entity, the conversion factors will vary widely. This can be a result of guaranteed compensation and productivity levels not being aligned. Variances can also result from physicians within the same specialty being on differing compensation plans.

TABLE 6-5   Conversion Factors Calculated Using Survey Data

Physician	Compensation	wRVUs	Ratio
Physician A	$661,935	11,297	$58.59
Physician B	$625,353	10,739	$58.23
Physician C	$517,349	9,091	$56.91
Physician D	$453,766	8,124	$55.85
Physician E	$604,885	10,428	$58.01
Physician F	$629,708	10,803	$58.29

©2013 Coker Group

Similar to the specific wRVU data, the actual ratio can be benchmarked as well. Many take the use of these benchmark ratios one step further and actually use them to develop a compensation model. This results in a consistent conversion factor regardless of the level of productivity for the physicians. Clearly, this is not the case in the above data. The use of conversion factors in developing compensation models based on wRVUs is further described in Chapter 4.

A ratio also can be calculated using collections and wRVUs (Table 6-6). This is done simply by replacing compensation with collections. Once again, this can be benchmarked and used in analyzing the performance of the practice. This ratio can be useful in determining the relationship between actual collections and the objective wRVU standard. When compared to benchmarks or even internally to other physicians, it may indicate trends that require further analysis.

TABLE 6-6   Data for Various Family Practice Physicians Employed by Same Physician Network

Physician	Compensation	wRVUs	Ratio
Physician A	$146,667	2,370	$61.89
Physician B	$179,843	3,114	$57.75
Physician C	$191,640	6,150	$31.16
Physician D	$198,818	4,079	$48.74
Physician E	$192,692	4,071	$47.33
Physician F	$211,528	4,270	$49.54
Physician G	$192,500	5,149	$37.39
Physician H	$229,144	4,807	$47.67
Physician I	$192,364	3,970	$48.46
Physician J	$315,956	6,136	$51.49

©2013 Coker Group

CONCLUSION

For the most part, using wRVUs in relation to productivity is a matter of obtaining useful information. This information can be used to better understand the performance of a physician or its use can be extended further to perform even more in-depth analysis of a medical practice.

The healthcare industry has evolved to a point that gross charges and collections, for a variety of reasons, are not as useful in assessing productivity. Currently, wRVUs appear to be the most objective productivity measure and their use continues to gain ground throughout the industry. As long as CMS works to maintain its relevancy and the appropriateness of the wRVU values assigned to each CPT code, this trend likely will continue.

Utilizing RVUs in Practice Management

In the previous chapters, we discussed the benefits of using relative value units (RVUs) to determine physician compensation and measure productivity. However, RVUs are not limited strictly to the productivity side of the equation; they also can be utilized effectively to manage costs, to set and negotiate favorable fee schedules with managed care organizations (MCOs), and to benchmark practice operations. A practice should have a thorough understanding of its costs to effectively manage its business and ensure financial viability. These aspects are discussed in this chapter.

COST MEASUREMENT AND ANALYSIS UTILIZING RVUS

Cost will need to include all outlays of cash and expenses that the revenue of the practice is expected to carry. Cost represents all facility expenses, staffing, malpractice, marketing, and all line items associated with overhead. In a medical practice, cost also includes all forms of physician compensation. Salaries, draws, bonuses, and other forms of compensation are also costs in that revenue must be generated so that funds are available to allow for compensation. It is recommended that such physician compensation and benefit-related costs be specifically separated on the practice's financial statements such that physician/non-physician cost comparisons may be performed reasonably. It is common to describe a practice in terms of its overhead, meaning the portion of revenue that is not paid to a physician. While this description is accurate, it falls short of being helpful in setting a pricing strategy, in understanding and controlling costs, or in payer contract negotiations.

A practice uses several measurements to evaluate and understand cost. These include but are not limited to cost per visit, cost per full-time equivalent (FTE) provider, cost per procedure, cost as a percentage of net revenue, and cost per RVU. All are appropriate ways to measure and analyze cost. However, RVU cost analyses enable a practice to consider procedure profitability or loss, set fee schedules based on cost, and negotiate managed care contracts based on cost.

Resource-based relative value scale (RBRVS) cost accounting enables a practice to estimate costs using relative value units to scale procedures and costs on a common basis. The cost per RVU can be calculated and, when multiplied by the RVU for each level of service, produces an estimate of the relative cost of providing services. The

Medicare RBRVS costing method is used to approximate the cost of delivering a level of service.

CALCULATION OF TOTAL COST PER RVU

To calculate total cost per RVU, begin with production measurement. Production equates to every patient- care service that the practice performs. Only patient services are included in a measurement of production because they are the production output of the practice. Many other services may be performed, such as assisting in referral or filing claims, but these services do not generate revenue.

It is important to capture every unit of production, even if there is no payment for the service; for example, a service that was not paid because of a payment policy rule. These patient-care services that do not have revenue associated with them are still part of the production of the practice because they consume resources in the form of time, supplies, and staffing.

Gathering production data begins by assembling data for every current procedural terminology (CPT) code that was performed by the practice during the same timeframe that the cost data spans, usually on a year-to-date basis. All services are gathered, regardless of whether they are paid. The frequency of each CPT code is collected as well. Care is taken not to over count services that are structured under a global fee. In most cases, it is most appropriate to capture the RVUs associated with the global fee and not additional value for specific services included in that global fee.

Once the CPT frequency data are gathered, the RVU for each CPT code is attached. The frequency of each CPT code is multiplied by the RVU for each CPT code and then the values of the RVUs are summed for each CPT code. This number represents the total production of the practice measured in RVUs. Note that we are referring here to RVUs in total, and that a measurement of work RVUs (wRVUs) may also be used as a measurement.

One of the most critical components in RVU analysis is accurate coding. Coding and proper documentation, a necessity to assure that revenue is appropriately recognized, starts with the education of the physician and staff. It also entails regular review of the coding procedures within the practice through an audit of the medical chart. Using a twofold approach, coding reviews should be completed (1) internally and (2) externally by a third party on a periodic basis to assure compliance. The primary purpose of most chart reviews is to assure compliance with Medicare and other guidelines. An additional benefit is the legitimate recognition of revenue through enhanced documentation or precise coding practices. Coding affects RVU analysis from a revenue standpoint, but also as it pertains to analyzing cost. Upcoding overstates the revenue while understating the cost. Undercoding understates revenue while overstating the cost. As will be addressed throughout this section, it is critical to calculate an accurate total cost per RVU in order to effectively manage the practice.

Another aspect of coding reviews can be the completion of a revenue analysis among the various providers within the practice to ascertain trends in coding and documentation. In a practice, physicians often see essentially the same type of patients, but may document these encounters differently via diagnostic coding procedures.

By conducting a periodic coding review, physicians can stay abreast of all the coding changes that occur. In addition, the practice should make every effort to obtain appropriate maximized revenue for services rendered.

With the production information, we can now calculate the total cost per RVU—the basis for all RVU cost analysis. It is the breakeven amount as it pertains to managed care contracting for those contracts that utilize RVUs and conversion factors by enabling the practice to compare cost per procedure to reimbursement per procedure.

A conversion factor is a dollar amount that is multiplied by the RVU to convert the RVU value into a fee for each CPT code. It is what both Medicare and some MCOs use as the basis for their fee schedule. Understanding the relationship between the total cost per RVU and conversion factor is critical to ensure that reimbursement covers overhead expenses and the practice can, in turn, generate a profit margin. If a practice were to accept a conversion factor or fee lower than the RVU, then the practice would essentially lose money.

As will be addressed in the managed care section, the conversion factor that has been used most predominantly is the Medicare conversion factor. The Medicare conversion factor has fluctuated over the past several years as indicated in Table 7-1. The fluctuation presents challenges when evaluating and setting fee schedules. When comparing with Medicare, it is critical that the practice use the Medicare conversion factor consistent with the same year's RVUs. For example, if a practice used the 2011 Medicare RVUs to measure production, then it must use the 2011 conversion factor for an accurate comparison with Medicare.

Two cost-per-procedure methods can be used to calculate total cost per RVU:

- Total cost per RVU
- The sum of the cost of the component RVUs.

Though the two methods produce different calculated costs, using them together can produce a cost range that the practice can use to ensure that the costs of delivering services are reimbursed adequately.

TABLE 7-1 Historical Medicare Conversion Factors[1]

Calendar Year	Factor
2008	$38.0870
2009	$36.0660
2010	$36.0791
2011	$33.9764
2012	$34.0376
2013	$34.0230

[1] http://www.ama-assn.org/resources/doc/rbrvs/cf-history.pdf.

Method One–Calculating Total Cost per RVU

The first method uses total relative value units to determine total cost per RVU. This is the formula for calculating the total cost per RVU:

$$\text{Total Cost per RVU} = \frac{\text{Total Expenses (Provider and Practice Expenses)}}{\text{Total RVUs}}$$

The product of this calculation is expressed as dollars per RVU and represents the average total cost per RVU.

Method Two—Calculating Total Cost per RVU Using the Sum of the Component Cost Per RVU

The second, more detailed RBRVS cost accounting method uses the sum of the component RVUs. These include work-related expense RVUs (wRVUs), practice expense-related RVUs (PE RVUs), and malpractice expense-related RVUs (MP RVUs). The values of RVUs are summed for each CPT code. This number represents the total production of the practice measured in RVUs.

- Calculating cost per wRVU

  The wRVU measures the provider's time and effort needed to deliver a level of service. Calculating the cost per wRVU enables a practice to determine a provider's total cost per wRVU. The calculation is shown in the following equation:

$$\text{Cost per Work RVU (wRVU)} = \frac{\text{Total Provider Expenses}}{\text{Total wRVUs}}$$

  It is important to determine and define provider costs (costs for both the physicians and midlevel providers). Provider compensation includes salary, bonuses, taxes, and all associated benefits. It does not include malpractice expense, however, since that is captured in the malpractice expense-related RVUs. Determining what is or is not a provider expense varies among practices. However, to get the most accurate cost per wRVU, any direct expense associated with a provider should be deemed part of provider compensation. By doing this, all other non-physician expenses are indirect expenses and are then deemed non-physician or overhead of the practice. This will enable the practice to more accurately measure overhead costs on an RVU basis.

- Calculating cost per Practice Expense RVU (PE RVU)

  The PE RVU measures the costs associated with delivering a level of service. It measures all the non-physician related expenses of the practice. These include all non-physician salary and benefits, supplies, billing, collections, and miscellaneous expenses—the remaining expenses after the provider expenses are determined as described in the preceding paragraph. The cost per PE RVU is calculated as shown in the following equation:

$$\text{Cost per Practice Expense RVU (PE RVU)} = \frac{\text{Total Practice Expenses}}{\text{Total PE RVUs}}$$

- Calculating cost per Malpractice Expense RVU (MP RVU)

The MP RVU is the malpractice cost associated with delivering a clinical service. The cost per MP RVU is calculated as shown the following equation:

$$\text{Cost per Malpractice Expense RVU (MP RVU)} = \frac{\text{Total Malpractice Expenses}}{\text{Total MP RVUs}}$$

After calculating the components, use the formula for calculating the total cost per RVU as shown in the following equation:

$$\text{Total Cost Per RVU} = (\text{wRVU x Cost/wRVU}) + (\text{PE RVU x Cost/PE RVU}) + (\text{MP RVU x Cost/MP RVU})$$

Information Required for Calculating Cost per RVU

The following information is required to calculate the cost per RVU:

- A production report of all CPT codes for a given period (preferably year-to-date)
- An income statement for the same period as the production report (preferably year-to-date)
- A spreadsheet software package
- The National Fee Schedule Relative Value File from CMS (download from http://www.cms.gov/Medicare/Medicare.html)

APPLYING TOTAL COST PER RVU DATA IN MANAGING THE PRACTICE

Now that the total cost per RVU data has been calculated, the question becomes: how does the practice utilize the data to better manage the practice? The following sections discuss some practical areas of application.

Establishing Fee Schedules for Managed Care Contracts

Practices have some flexibility when setting fee schedules with MCOs. Unlike Medicare, MCOs employ a variety of payment methodologies. It is the responsibility of the practice to develop a method to evaluate payer fee schedules that allows a practice to track and understand the different nuances each possess. By establishing a sound and practical methodology, the practice will be able to ensure appropriate reimbursement. However, due to the competition, many practices follow a market-driven approach that ties fees to the perceived skills and respective charges found in the marketplace. Under a market-driven approach, fees stay current with industry trends as they emerge in the local community. This method also relies partially on the assumption that patients are price-sensitive and are aware of cost differences among physician. This seems to be an emerging trend given the availability of information through the Internet. While this is the case and should factor into establishing an appropriate fee schedule, the practice must focus on ensuring that the reimbursement covers the practice overhead.

However, many practices feel powerless when thinking about payer contracting and establishing fee schedules. Some believe they must take what the payer is offering or risk seeing their patient base dwindle. This is especially prevalent in smaller practices that have little or no leverage in the marketplace. Some do not know what rates to ask for at the negotiating table. In addition, pay-for-performance is a becoming a reality in the market that will have a greater impact on the amount of reimbursement the practice will receive. Therefore, it is imperative that a practice be able to measure costs for any procedure or service delivered by a provider in order to ensure that the cost to deliver the level of service is covered by the level of reimbursement received. To ensure financial viability, it is critical to determine what the breakeven amount is for a level of service or, in other words, when "total cost equals total reimbursement" for a level of service or procedure.

The cost per procedure utilizing the RVU methodology is an effective tool that enables a practice to understand the relationship between the cost to produce a level of service and the reimbursement needed to cover those costs. By understanding the costs per procedure through RVU utilization, the practice can make more informed business decisions when setting fees and negotiating with MCOs. The total cost per RVU is the breakeven amount for a fee schedule based on RVUs and conversion factors.

As noted by Kathryn Glass in *RVUs: Application for Medical Practice Success,* one method to determine the total cost per RVU is by developing a cost-based fee schedule. By utilizing this method, a practice is able to determine a fee schedule based on the cost of each CPT code. In other words, it allows the practice to compare cost per procedure to reimbursement per procedure, necessary not only to cover the costs but to ensure profitability, as well.[1]

In Table 7-2, total cost per RVU is $39.86. To determine the cost per CPT code, simply multiply total cost per RVU, or $39.86, by the total RVUs per CPT code as defined by the American Medical Association.

Remember, this determines the breakeven amount when establishing a fee schedule. The practice would want to build in a profit margin across the entire fee schedule and negotiate that amount with the MCOs. However, a uniform fee schedule must be set for all patients. Therefore, the practice needs to ensure that the profit margin multiplier creates a fee schedule that covers all managed care contracted fees, in addition to all contractual adjustments and write-offs. In this example, a profit margin multiplier of 200% was used. Even though there are different methodologies for determining a fee schedule, the following premise must be understood and followed:

The negotiated fee amount for any managed care contract must be greater than the cost-based fee amount.

There are various types of managed care contracts: those based on a percentage of Medicare, discounted fee-for-service, proprietary, capitation, or fixed conversion factors/RBRVS RVU. Discounted fee-for-service (or paying a percentage of charges) and capitation are becoming less prevalent in most regions of the country. Negotiating from a total cost per RVU perspective allows the practice

---

[1] Glass, Kathryn P. RVUs: Application for Medical Practice Success, 2nd Ed. (Denver: Medical Group Management Association, 2008), 100-102.

CPT Code	Description	Frequency	2013 TRVUs	TRVUs	Cost per CPT Code	Profit Margin Multiplier	Fee per Procedure
99211	Office/outpatient visit, est	12,000	0.60	7,200	$23.91	200%	$48
99212	Office/outpatient visit, est	20,000	1.29	25,800	$51.41	200%	$103
99213	Office/outpatient visit, est	30,000	2.13	63,900	$84.90	200%	$168
99214	Office/outpatient visit, est	25,000	3.13	78,250	$124.76	200%	$250
99215	Office/outpatient visit, est	15,000	4.20	-63,000	$167.41	200%	$335
				238,150			

TABLE 7-2   E&M Cost-Based Fee Schedule

Total Practice Cost $9,493,260

Total Cost per RVU $-39.86

Profit Margin Multiplier   200%

Cost per CPT Code = Total Cost/RVU x total RVU per CPT Code
   ($39.86 x Col D)

to negotiate fee schedules in a more knowledgeable, effective, and practical way. Therefore, the next section will focus on understanding and negotiating fee schedules by using total cost per RVU in the following three areas: percent of Medicare; fixed conversion factor and RBRVS RVUs for a given year, and proprietary.

Evaluating MCO Fees based on a Percentage of the Medicare Fee Schedule

One of the most prevalent ways to negotiate a fee schedule with an MCO is to use a percentage of Medicare, often referred to as a Medicare multiplier. It is done using one of two methods.

The first method is to multiply the Medicare allowable fee by a percentage, or multiplier. For example,

CPT code Medicare allowable: $100 X 130% = $130

The second method is to multiply the Medicare conversion factor by the multiplier:

2013 Medicare conversion factor: $34.0230 X 130% = $45,90402

The new conversion factor of $45.90402 is then multiplied by the current year RVUs per CPT code in order to establish the contracted fee schedule.

Now that the value and importance of understanding total cost per RVU has been established, using a multiplier of the Medicare conversion factor and comparing it to total cost per RVU has more practical application in negotiating managed care contracts. This is because it enables the practice to compare its total costs per RVU to the Medicare conversion factor. In other words, it allows the practice to analyze the impact of the practice costs as it relates to the Medicare conversion factor.

A practice that accepts Medicare patients cannot negotiate the fee schedule with Medicare. Therefore, the volume of Medicare patients can have a negative

TABLE 7-3   Comparing Practice Costs as a Percentage of the Medicare Fee Schedule

	2007	2008	2013
Practice A total cost RVU	$46.67	$49.55	$39.86
Medicare conversion factor	37.8975	38.0870	34.02
Total cost per RVU as percentage of Medicare CF	123.15%	130.10%	117.17%

impact on the practice with regard to covering practice overhead expenses. It is critical for a practice to compare the total practice costs with the reimbursement from Medicare in order to understand the impact. If total cost per RVU is greater than the Medicare conversion factor, an extra percentage should be factored in when negotiating a fee schedule with an MCO in order to compensate for the short-fall and cover the practice overhead.[2]

In Table 7-3, the 2013 total cost per RVU is $39.86 as compared to the Medicare conversion factor of $34.02. Expressed as a percentage of Medicare, the total cost per RVU is 117.17% of Medicare. As we discussed in the previous sections, the breakeven cost for the practice is the total cost per RVU when utilizing RVUs and conversion factors. As demonstrated in this particular case, the practice is losing money on Medicare since the Medicare conversion factor of $34.02 is less than the total cost per RVU of $39.86. Therefore, to compensate for this loss and ensure the financial viability of the practice, all MCO contracts need to be negotiated at a rate higher than 117.17% to break even.[3] To make a profit, an additional percentage, or profit multiplier, needs to be built in. In addition, the practice may consider decreasing Medicare volume as well if they are not able to successfully negotiate the higher MCO rates.

This analysis also serves as a useful tool for the practice as it indicates that the total cost per RVU has an upward trend over the previous two years, signaling that more analyses of expenses may be warranted to pinpoint areas for further cost reduction.

The drawback of utilizing the percentage of Medicare methodology for setting fees is that the Medicare conversion factor and RBRVS RVUs vary from year to year. Therefore, the fee schedule will fluctuate from year to year as well. Given this volatility, it is essential that the practice evaluate the impact of the new Medicare fee schedule as soon as the new fee schedule information is made available in order to determine the impact on the practice and to determine if the contract needs to be renegotiated with the MCO.

Evaluating MCO Fees Based on a Fixed Conversion Factor and RBRVS RVUs for a Given Year

To avoid the fluctuations in fee schedules based on a percentage of Medicare, a practice may consider negotiating a fee schedule with an MCO with a fixed conversion factor, or conversion factors, if the MCO pays different conversion factors

[2] Ibid, 131.
[3] Ibid, 132.

TABLE 7-4 Historical Medicare Conversion Factors	
Calendar Year	**Factor**
2006	$37.8950
2007	$37.8950
2008	$38.0870
2009	$36.0660

for CPT code ranges and RBRVS RVUs for a given year.[4] Table 7-4 shows the fluctuations over the past four years.

Different specialties can have very different overhead structures. Therefore, segmenting the CPT codes into the specialty ranges can provide the practice even more leverage and control in ensuring that overhead expenses, or total cost per RVU, are covered.

By establishing a fixed methodology that is not tied to Medicare, the fee schedule does not fluctuate year after year. However, it is critical that the practice continue to monitor the total cost per RVU to determine if expenses are trending upward. If they are and cannot be reduced further, the practice will need to renegotiate the contract with the MCO to ensure that overhead costs are covered and an acceptable profit margin is realized.

Evaluating MCO Fees Based on a Proprietary Fee Schedule

Some MCOs do not offer a fee schedule based conversion factors; they simply provide their own fee schedule to the practice.[5] Most of the time (and this applies in all cases obtaining the fee schedule regardless of what method is used) the MCO gives only a limited number of fees—usually the evaluation and management (E&M) codes and a limited number of procedure codes. Though frustrating, it is critical to be persistent in obtaining the fee schedule. In what other business do you have to "trust" the payer so unconditionally? Fortunately, significant efforts are being made to change this practice and thus improve the process and relationship with the MCOs. Most often, practices have to keep submitting a limited number of fees in order to obtain the necessary information. It is important to take the top cost based on what generates 80% to 85% of the volume within the practice and obtain the fees.

Once the proprietary fee schedule is received, several methods of comparison can be used. The first, as discussed above, is to compare the fees with the Medicare allowable fees and conversion factor. This should be done in a spread- sheet format or preferably an analytical software program within your practice management information system. If the MCO does not provide the conversion factor, it is easily calculated by dividing the fee amount by the total RVUs for that procedure. The same methodology discussed above in the previous sections then applies: the

---

[4] Ibid, 126.
[5] Ibid, 122.

conversion factor must be greater than the total cost per RVU to ensure profitability.

In summary, regardless of the methodology applied, using RVUs to evaluate costs and then compare to the conversion factors can ensure the financial viability of the practice. In addition, it is important that the practice track the different MCO contracts. If the percentage of Medicare fee schedule methodology is used, it is critical to track both the RVUs and the conversion factor from year to year. A simple spreadsheet is a useful tool to accomplish this.

Benchmarking Utilizing Total Cost per RVU

Benchmarks are statistical comparisons that form economic standards on which to compare and measure the actual performance results of a practice. Benchmarks, therefore, are the methodology to gauge practice performance against independent standards. Benchmarks, when used within reason, are advantageous as a comparative analysis and should be used as primary comparisons against actual performance.

Benchmarks are not emphatically correct and, therefore, should be used conservatively; they should not generate overreaction. They are compiled from various sources with worthy means on which to base them, but often are unscientific compilations of data. The best utilization of benchmarking is in an ongoing process that allows the use of an independent standard to compare productivity, expenses, and certain quality measures.

Benchmarking is a way to establish targeted performance and is an excellent tool with which to monitor business/management results. Benchmarking allows for objective, measurable performance standards to be compared against performance as a way to pinpoint trends and receive early warning signals that may be indications of strength or weakness.

A key point to note is that benchmarking is the use of external sources to compare internal performance. While it is important to measure performance against internal standards, such as the budget and the previous year's performance, it is also beneficial to use external standards. Otherwise, performance that seems beneficial may merely be acceptable. Even if the performance is adequate, it is essential to consider external sources or standards for comparison in pursuit of experience and knowledge of the business. Some examples of external sources include:

- Medical Group Management Association (www.mgma.com)
- American Medical Association (www.ama-assn.org)
- Center for Healthcare Industry Performance Studies (http://openlibrary.org/a/OL3062658A/Center-for-Healthcare-Industry-Performance-Studies)
- American Medical Group Association (www.amga.org)
- Medical Economics (http://medicaleconomics.modernmedicine.com)
- Practice Support Resources, Inc. (http://www.practicesupport.com)
- Individual research initiatives via consulting firms

Whatever the source of the benchmarks, it is essential to understand the data. The benchmarks should be accompanied by a thorough explanation of how the data were compiled and of what the data consists. For benchmarking to be credible, the data must be comparative, which is usually the greatest challenge in terms of benchmarking comparisons within the medical practice. These are the basic problems that surface when turning to external resources, which demand close analysis and definition of the external benchmarking sources. Once the definitions are ascertained, numbers usually can be adjusted to reflect somewhat comparable, albeit functional, data on which to compare and benchmark.

It is essential to define benchmarking comparisons and to use them consistently. There are several different indicators with regard to analyzing expenses. These include:

- Cost per procedure;
- Cost as a percentage of net revenue;
- Cost per full time equivalent (FTE); and
- Total cost per RVU.

While all comparisons are valid and should be utilized, using RVUs for benchmarking is a less-complex comparison because RVUs are standardized units of measure. They allow for the comparison of one level of service to another, and the assigned units attempt to better equalize the complexity and value of one CPT code to another. As has been discussed throughout this chapter, by calculating the total cost per RVU and then comparing it the conversion factor, the practice is able to ensure that the reimbursement rate that it is receiving and/or negotiating with a MCO covers the overhead expenses and ensures they are making a reasonable profit.

Another area of benchmarking that has an effect on cost is coding. We established earlier that ensuring an appropriate level of coding has a direct impact on calculating an accurate total cost per RVU. Not doing so will lead to understating or overstating total cost per RVU. Furthermore, if it is understated, this could have a negative impact on the practice. For example, negotiating a MCO contract with an understated total cost RVU could result in negotiating a fee that is not able to accurately cover overhead expenses. Therefore, it is beneficial to benchmark a level of coding to certain standards. Often with E&M codes, the best distribution is thought to be somewhat of a bell curve. That is, there will be fewer occurrences at either end of the E&M codes, with the majority of coding occurring at levels two, three, and four. Although not always the case (nor always the right way), the bell curve can give a basic benchmark from which to manage and monitor performance.

Benchmarks should be used regularly, perhaps as often as weekly or daily. Several prerequisites ensure success in the accumulation of data:

- The information should be accurately compiled;
- Outside information should be provided from recognized and established sources;

- The information should be used as a tool for learning and enabling change; and
- The organization must be committed to consistently using the data.

To summarize benchmarking, several different benchmarking marking techniques can be used to measure performance and analyze cost.

A combination of these may be the best approach. There is no one perfect benchmark; however, because total cost RVU offers a standardized measure, it tends to level the playing field in measuring one level of service against another, and allows a powerful method to identify the breakeven amount for a given service.

CONCLUSION

Physicians and practice administrators constantly struggle to maintain both profitability and a competitive edge in the ever-changing healthcare marketplace. In order to not only survive but to thrive, it is critical to understand the costs associated with managing the practice. Determining the total cost per RVU provides a useful statistical and objective measure. RVU cost analysis enables a practice to analyze procedure profitability or loss, set fee schedules based on cost, and negotiate favorable managed-care contracts. It provides a standard unit of measure that produces valuable data about the resources that are used and work expended in the delivery of services that can then be used to help maintain profitability.

RVUs and ACOs/CINs

As our healthcare industry moves into the era of "accountable care," the utilization of RVUs will take on a new dynamic. The rising cost of healthcare is a national crisis and all key players—physicians, hospitals, employers, insurance companies, and consumers—are facing unprecedented challenges as they attempt to control expenses in the current environment. With the advent of the affordable care act (ACA), a.k.a. the Patient Protection and Affordable Care Act (PPACA), healthcare quality and costs alike are taking on much greater emphasis than ever before (at least in the entire reimbursement paradigm). Note: The Affordable Care Act (H.R.3590) was passed by Congress and then signed into law by the President on March 23, 2010. On June 28, 2012 the Supreme Court rendered a final decision to uphold the healthcare law. The intent of the act was to improve the experience of care for individuals, the health of populations and lowering per capita costs.

While RVUs clearly are a unit of productivity measurement and therefore somewhat inconsistent with the premise of accountable care, with its emphasis on quality outcomes and lower costs, they will still have a role in the overall delivery system and accountability functions.

First, RVUs will continue to be a part of the delivery system under accountable care because fee-for-service reimbursement will not totally go away. Indeed, the prospect of being paid based upon certain levels of productivity will continue. Second, RVUs will continue to be a part of the system under accountable care because of their flexibility. By this we mean that units of value (which again in essence is all that an RVU is attempting to be) can still be derived. For example, based on certain levels of performance and quality outcomes, RVUs could be awarded under such basis as opposed to sheer fee-for-service productivity. This likewise could apply within the structure for cost savings.

Finally, RVUs will continue to be a part of the equation—even in the accountable care era—because they are by far the best methodology for computing compensation due providers in an employed or contracted setting.

As we delve into the entire concept of accountable care in this chapter, we consider how RVUs are affected by these newly formed accountable care entities and how they will affect RVUs going forward. Specifically, we will discuss the concepts of accountable care organizations (ACOs) and clinically integrated organizations or clinically integrated networks (CIOs/CINs). These are specific consortiums that have been initiated as a result of the ACA and as such, will form a new dynamic for providers managing large groups of populations (i.e., "population health management" concepts). For purposes of our discussion in this chapter, we refer to ACOs as essentially the CMS/Medicare model for reimbursement, while CIOs/CINs are the private sector model for reimbursement. Many CIOs/CINs are a result of initial formations of PHOs and IPAs and are managing large groups of populations in conjunction with private payers.

Thus, the entire concept of ACOs/CIOs/CINs is very much a part of the healthcare landscape within the concepts and purviews of relative value units.

OVERVIEW OF THE CURRENT HEALTHCARE LANDSCAPE

While healthcare reform and accountable care are here to stay, many challenges are associated with its implementation, including:

- Uncertain fiscal ramifications;
- Uncertainty of exactly how ACOs and CIOs will function;
- Lack of clarity and IT infrastructure;
- The fact that most Americans still get medical care from small practices;
- Expanded infrastructure required to drive quality outcomes;
- Physician/hospital alignment is essential; and
- Integration required to give effect to value-based purchasing.

Thus, the changes occurring are unprecedented. Hospitals, physicians and others in the healthcare industry will require constant assessment and evaluation of their entire care delivery processes in order to respond to the new reimbursement structures. Moreover, this will have a significant effect on the way RVUs are considered in the context of operations, evaluations, and overall processes within the healthcare delivery system.

Clinical integration is one of the major parts of the continuum going forward. Any integrated delivery system must have a process in place that includes the communication and sharing of clinical data—clinical integration. Accountable care era structures focus on delivering care in a coordinated/integrated system, stressing streamlined services across patient care models to achieve efficiencies in quality. This entails changing paradigms. Such paradigms include those outlined in Figure 8-1:

FIGURE 8-1	
From	**To**
Care management in silos	Integrated care management
Episodes of care	Coordination of care
Utilization management	Proper care at the appropriate place and time
Caring for sick people	Preventative care (keeping people well)
Production (volume)	Performance (value)
Disjointed provider base	ACOs and CINs

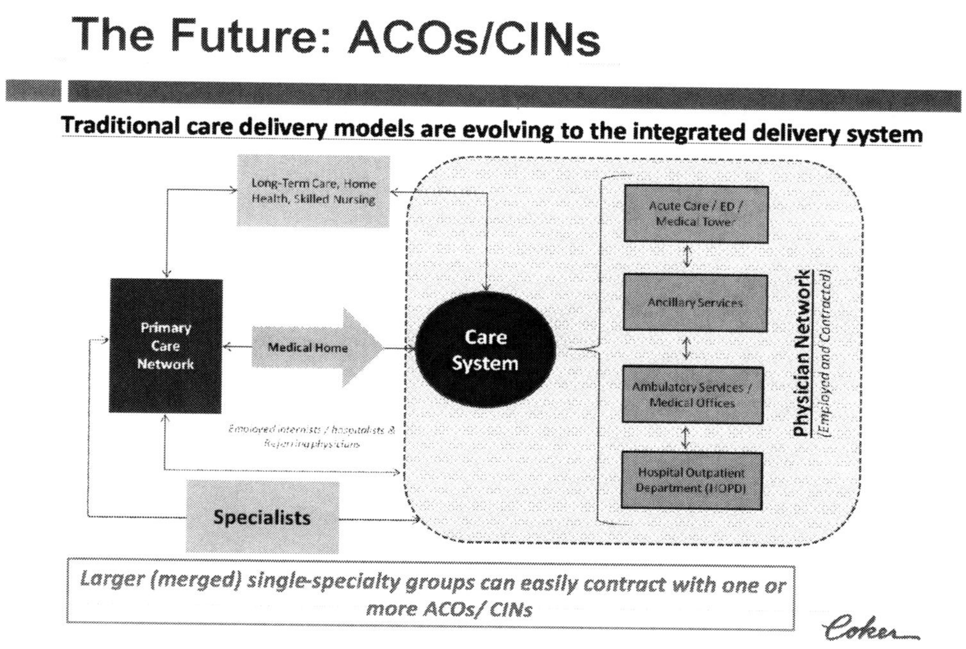

The Future: ACOs/CINs

Traditional care delivery models are evolving to the integrated delivery system

FIGURE 8-2

While some of these traits do not directly influence RVUs, some are very much a part of the consideration of RVUs in the management and overall structuring of medical practices. Of course, the most notable shift above is the shift from a sheer production and volume model to a performance- and value-based model. As stated earlier however, we are not convinced that RVUs will be totally abandoned. There still will be a partial fee-for-service payment, RVUs will continue to be a part of the system under accountable care because of the flexibility, and they are by far the best methodology for computing compensation due providers in an employed or contracted setting.

We believe the future of ACOs, CINs and related entities will look something like the diagram in Figure 8-2.

Traditional care delivery models that are focused on silos of care independent of each other will no longer be the case. Care coordination and population health management are considered the future of our American healthcare delivery system. Again, where do RVU fit into these structures? While they will not have as great of an impact as they once had, we believe they clearly will still be a major part of the overall management and administrative (and yes indeed, performance evaluation) structure.

ACOS, CIOS, AND RELATED MODELS

To fully understand the impact of the new accountable care era structures on RVUs, we should take a step back and consider specific characteristics of ACOs, CIOs, and related models.

FIGURE 8-3 CONTEMPORARY "ACCOUNTABLE CARE ERA" ALIGNMENT MODELS
Alignment is a foundation to respond to the changing paradigm.

Strategy	Basic Concept	Compensation Framework
Patient-Centered Medical Homes	• Team of providers and medical individuals collaborating to provide patient-centric care in a focused ambulatory care environment; can be part of ACO/CIN model	• Varying incentives based on contractual relationships with payers
Quality Collaboratives	• Consortium of providers focused on furthering the quality outcomes for a defined population	• Internal or external funding sources determine scope and structure of available funds
Clinically Integrated Networks (or Organizations)	• Interdependent healthcare facilities form a network with providers that collaboratively develop and sustain clinical initiatives	• Incentive (i.e., at-risk) compensation based on achievement of pre-determined measures
Accountable Care Organizations (ACOs)	• Participating hospitals, providers, and other healthcare professionals collaborating to deliver quality and cost effective care to Medicare (and other) patient populations	• Incentive (and punitive) financial impacts based on cost savings and quality

First, contemporary accountable care alignment models entail new structures and new reimbursement paradigms. Figure 8-3 illustrates primary accountable care era alignment models, their basic concepts, and corresponding compensation framework.

Thus, we see that the new models focus on things that are somewhat different than previously. Moreover, compensation frameworks are also quite different and there is no specific mention of RVUs as being the primary model of compensation recognition in any of these structures. However, as we have already stated, fee-for-service will continue to have some influence and even if it ultimately takes a back seat to payment based on quality and cost containments, RVUs should always be a methodology for comparing one provider to another relative to performance under specific metrics and criteria. Historically, that performance has been measured in production units and thus RVUs are reflective of such. In the future, RVUs may well be more related to the measurement or metrics of performance tied to standards of quality outcomes and cost containment as opposed to sheer productivity. Nonetheless, they will have a function going forward as a method of measure of performance.

The concept of clinically integrated organizations (or networks) is illustrated in Figure 8-4.

This illustrates the concepts of clinically integrated organizations or networks (CIOs/CINs) in that a consortium of providers band together to form the CIO/CIN which in turn will become the contracting vehicle with commercial payers. In many instances, the Medicare ACO also looks and feels the same in terms of a consortium of providers coming together to work and serve Medicare patients.

Thus, clinical integration and clinically integrated entities will become a major part of the healthcare landscape going forward. RVUs will need to be responsive to

FIGURE 8-4   Clinically Integrated Networks

- Primary focus of CIN (also referred to as Clinically Integrated Organization [CIO]) is to create a high degree of interdependence among participating providers.
- Network of interdependent healthcare facilities and providers that collaboratively develop and sustain clinical initiatives on an ongoing basis through a centralized, coordinated strategy
  - Patient-centric
  - Structures may vary from provider-to-provider
  - Heavily reliant on robust IT infrastructure
- Physician involvement necessary
  - Governance
  - Quality improvement initiatives
  - Establishing reliable metrics
  - Personnel management & training
  - Overseeing compliance across network
  - Centralized contracting

Source: Washington Healthcare News, *"Meeting the Challenge of Healthcare Reform: The Clinically Integrated Network,"* March 2012

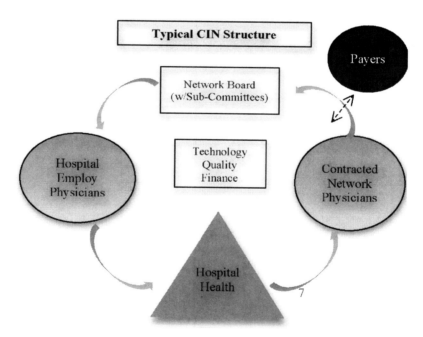

these new entities and will be a major factor in how performance is measured and evaluated—just as they are today in a virtually totally fee-for-service productivity-based environment.

OVERVIEW AND PURPOSE OF CINS

Why are CINs becoming so popular and what are the overarching principles that drive them? They are a result of the "accountable care era" and by definition, are focused on the commercial payer market (whereas in many people's vernacular, ACOs are focused upon the Medicare/CMS product). Like ACOs, CINs, also referred to as clinically integrated organizations (CIOs), are designed to address the movement toward reimbursed based on improved quality and efficiency of care, utilization of evidence-based data for performance improvement, and ultimately a contract among payers and providers that aligns financial and clinical incentives. There are notable differences between CINs and ACOs as the regulations are specific that govern ACOs and of course are applicable to government payer reimbursement, whereas CINs are focused on the private marketplace and thus entail more flexibility and less regulation.

Although both CINs and ACOs meet these criteria, they also have notable differences in what governs them. As Medicare/CMS models, ACOs are subject to regulatory guidelines, which can mean extreme ramifications, while CINs relate to the private marketplace and are more flexible and less regulated.

Reimbursement Paradigm

The reimbursement paradigm is changing, as Figure 8-5 illustrates.

FIGURE 8–5	Accountable Care Paradigm					
Reimbursement Paradigm Is Changing						
Less Focus on Productivity	Sharing of Savings	Risk Sharing	Quality Collaboratives	Bundled Payments (OBs Under Global Payment for Years)	Blended Payments	Capitation (CMS Pioneer Model, Year 3 and Commercial ACOs)

[1] Coker Group, *Developing an Effective Clinically Integrated Network—Part One*, April 2013.

Reading from left to right, this chart illustrates that clearly, productivity-based reimbursement exists but the structures are moving at a somewhat accelerated pace toward payments tied to quality, cost savings, and ultimately, a form of blended and/or bundled payments. It is important for physicians and hospitals (and for that matter, all providers of healthcare) to work together, especially if the ultimate end-game is bundled or blended reimbursement. How this affects RVUs (and more specifically, RVUs used to measure productivity and compensation) is not fully determined yet. Clearly, to the extent that productivity and fee-for-service compensation and reimbursement still exists (and indeed, we believe it will exist to a large extent going forward), RVUs will be important. To the extent that the reimbursement changes, we still believe RVUs will be a critical component because with the effect of bundled reimbursement, productivity may well be a major basis upon which the allocation of bundled or blended payments are distributed among several providers.

Thus, it is essential for physicians/hospitals and other providers to collaborate, if not to fully integrate. Every hospital/health system in the United States should have an alignment strategy that includes various forms of collaboration/affiliation with physician groups. In many instances, this has taken the form of full employment (W-2), but it also can be an independent contractor relationship (i.e., IRS Form 1099), usually formalized through PSAs and/or management services agreements (MSAs). Regardless of the level and form of alignment, CINs/CIOs must exhibit the characteristics of physicians and hospitals working together through an affiliated model. The changing reimbursement paradigm will accommodate such structures; a bundled and/or blended payment structure would be challenged to accommodate reimbursing physicians who, for example, are not aligned with hospitals.[1]

Clinical Integration Focus

By definition, clinical integration is a "qualified clinically integrated arrangement" to provide physician services in which: all physicians who participate in "active and ongoing program to evaluate and modify the practice patterns by the network's physician participants and create a high degree of interdependence and cooperation among the physicians to control costs and ensure quality"[2] of services provided through the arrangement; and, any agreement concerning price or other terms or conditions of dealing entered into by or within the arrangement is reasonably necessary to obtain significant efficiencies through the joint arrangement.

In the purest sense, clinical integration entails providers working together to share information primarily centered on functional clinical data. The goal is to not only deliver the best possible care, but to do so with the most efficiency and lowest cost. A successful component of clinical integration is an information technology infrastructure that accommodates the ability to have a data repository of such clinical data. This is probably the greatest single driver of physician groups and health systems consolidating, as the cost of information technology is so high without such integration, it would be difficult to formulate a successful clinically integrated repository structure. Clinical integration helps complete the process of building data across a continuum of healthcare providers, including physician practices, hospitals and health systems, allied providers, diagnostic providers, etc.

Formulating a Clinically Integrated Network

The CIN comprises a grouping of interdependent healthcare providers working collaboratively with the foundation of clinically integrated data. Such entities form the basis for negotiating with payers and as such, become the vehicle for reimbursement. Indeed, many CINs actually are the recipients of payments from the private payers. RVUs will continue to be important, even under this new reimbursement structure. RVUs are a measurement of productivity; however, they also can be a way to define other areas of performance. While more subjective than true RVUs tied to CPT code values, there are ways to formulate RVU totals under other foundations or bases.

---

[1] In this instance, by alignment we are referring to some form of contractual agreement such as an employment contract, PSA, and/or MSA.

[2] Statements of Antitrust Enforcement Policy in Health Care by the FTC and the U.S. Department of Justice, Statement 8, http://www.ftc.gov/reports/hlth3s.htm#8. July 21, 2013.

For example, certain areas of quality measure and outcomes could be assigned RVU values. While these will not have the standards that CPT code-based RVU values do, if applied consistently and if good clinical outcomes data are existent, this will be possible over time. Thus, we view the next generation of RVUs being based upon a blended derivation as not much different than the way reimbursement will actually be paid. In other words, if we are looking at a CIN being paid based on a combination of productivity (i.e., fee-for-service, quality outcomes, cost controls, and patient satisfaction), all of these things could ultimately become standardized within the measurement and assignment of RVU values.

Figure 8-6 illustrates a possibility.

FIGURE 8-6	
Provider Performance	**Total RVUs**
RVUs (Based Upon CPT Codes)	
RVUs (Assigned Based Upon)	
1. Quality Outcomes	
2. Cost Controls	
3. Patient Satisfaction	

This basic illustration provides an indication of how RVUs could be used going forward under a blended payment reimbursement structure. Simply stated, RVUs could be developed as a standard for being assigned based on certain levels of patient satisfaction, quality outcomes, and cost savings. With fee-for-service productivity still very much a part of the anticipated new reimbursement structures, the ability to assign them based upon their relative values tied to CPT codes will still apply. The following figure summarizes key factors that should influence the establishment of a CIN.

FIGURE 8-7	Key Factors Existent to Establish a CIN[1]
Clearly-defined goals and objectives of entity	Utilizes resources currently available within the organizational consortium to build CIN
Emphasis on utilization of physician-driven model	Program designed to meet consumer healthcare needs of service area of CIN
Process initiated with modest clinical metrics, maturing as the process and CIN develops (with both experience and success)	Establish clinical protocols covering a large continuum of care (inpatient, outpatient/ambulatory, home care, skilled nursing functions, etc.)
Commitment of an investment in an effective infrastructure (especially IT) to electronically measure performance, compared against benchmarks and targeting needed improvements	Establish effective communication among providers, employers and other participants (including third-party payer contractors)

[1] Coker Group, *Developing an Effective Clinically Integrated Network—Part One*, April, 2013

As we consider those factors listed in Figure 8-7, the effect of RVUs will still be very relevant to these levels of performance.

Hypothetical CIN Structure

Figure 8-8 illustrates such a structure.

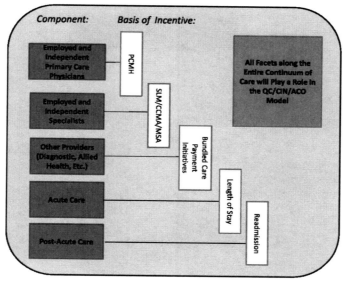

FIGURE 8-8
[1] Coker Group, April, 2013, *Developing an Effective Clinically Integrated Network—Part One,* April, 2013

The figure illustrates the importance of all of the payers adding to the continuum of care. No matter what the type of reimbursement or even the initial contact of the provider with the patient (for example, perhaps it would be within a patient-centered medical home, as illustrated in the above figure), the importance of a basis of the incentive to be paid is overarching. This illustration shows that the continuum of providers all formulate the required groups in order to effectuate a successful CIN (or for that matter, a CMS-regulated ACO). The key components to form the CIN not only apply to an acute-care hospital, but a cross-section of physicians specialties, including primary care, subspecialists, and specialists. Figure 8-9 (next page) illustrates how both clinically integrated networks and accountable care organizations might function over a full continuum of care/providers.

Payment Approaches

Earlier in this chapter we touched on and referred to various approaches for reimbursement. It appears that CINs (and ACOs also) will have two major approaches to payment. The first is a combination of fee-for-service and shared savings. Providers will still be paid largely on a fee-for-service basis and yet there will be a significant extra benefit realized through a shared savings process. We believe the shared savings process will be in the form of bonus payments that are tied to lower-than-expected cost performance while maintaining high standards of quality and outcomes. The second methodology is more so tied to a management of entire population-based entities. Population health management is indeed a

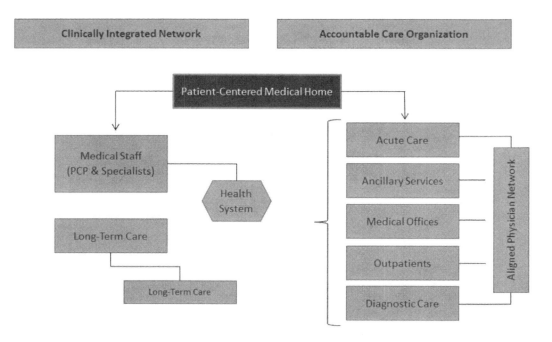

FIGURE 8-9

buzz term that is pervasive throughout the healthcare industry. Being able to manage the health of large groupings of populations is not a new concept. In fact, this has existed ever since the beginning of group health insurance. Nonetheless, in the context of the accountable care era, it will take on a whole new role and in many respects we believe very similar to what was tried in the '80s and '90s under capitated structures.

Capitation may return, though we believe it will be more so tied to a combination of fee-for-service and shared savings programs with the latter based on the three criteria noted earlier (quality outcomes, cost savings, and patient satisfaction). By managing an entire population of patients, the ability to truly affect care and lower costs will have to be done through a coordinated care delivery system, meaning that all providers must be involved and must be incented accordingly.

Providing payment incentives that allow for such could fundamentally change the underlying incentives and as a result, could have a major effect on how RVUs are assigned and monitored (already illustrated above in Figure 8-6). We must point out, however, that these programs are unproven and RVUs as a part of the overall quantification of performance are likewise far from defined. As a matter of fact, we have decided not to go further in any form of definition as to how RVUs would be accumulated because it such a relatively new concept and untried. However, the basic principles—the fundamental concepts that says that RVUs can be still used as a means to measure total physician performance, yet it no longer just be tied to fee-for-service production and the number of CPT codes garnered, is the overarching point and take away from this chapter.

SUMMARY

The entire accountable care era process is going through tremendous changes and adjustments and, while RVUs may not have the relevance that they have had in the past, we believe they will still be important to the overall determination of provider—and more specifically, physician and mid-level provider—performance.

Increasing Productivity via wRVU Measurements

Perhaps one of the best ways to demonstrate how productivity can be increased is by giving real-life examples. This chapter focuses on the ways one large group of physicians, associated with the Greater Baltimore Medical Center, Baltimore, Maryland, has increased productivity through the work-only component of relative value unit (wRVU) measurements. Based on his leadership role as vice-president of Greater Baltimore Medical Associates, Steven K. Twaddle, a Fellow of the American College of Medical Practice Executives, provided the following information.

OVERVIEW OF THE ORGANIZATION

Greater Baltimore Medical Associates is a hospital-based physician group associated with the Greater Baltimore Medical Center (GBMC). GBMC, a regional 335-bed medical center located on the north side of Baltimore, handles more than 26,700 inpatient cases and approximately 60,000 emergency visits annually. More than 200 of its physicians are employed through Greater Baltimore Medical Associates (GBMA), a division of GBMC, and practice in 41 separate practices supported by 400 full-time equivalent (FTE) support staff. GBMA features a diverse collection of practices in a number of different specialties, including Internal Medicine, Family Practice, Pediatrics, Obstetrics and Gynecology (OB/GYN), General and Specialty Surgery, and Oncology.

GBMC and its physicians have long been recognized for outstanding quality and personalized service within the community. Over the past decade, *U.S. News & World Report* has repeatedly cited the medical center as one of "America's Best Hospitals" in several areas of service. Additionally, *Baltimore Magazine's* annual "Top Doctors" edition consistently recognizes more members of GBMC's medical staff than any other hospital in the state.

In 2006, GBMC took unified actions to structure GBMA-employed physicians into viable categories representative of internal/external hospital services. Originally, the organization's investment per employed physician was well below the Medical Group Management Association (MGMA) 25th percentile per FTE. Today, the investment is closer to MGMA's median value for similar groups in a hospital-owned integrated delivery system (IDS).

GBMC Physicians, LLC, was formed in 2008 to be part of GBMC Healthcare, Inc., and ultimately not directly run by the GBMC hospital. The organization has separate officers, facilities, staff, and board of directors. It consists of Internal Medicine, Family Practice, OB/GYN, Pediatric, Geriatric, Subspecialty, and Surgical practices.

PHYSICIANS

A measure of a physician's production is wRVU, as discussed in prior chapters. Combined with other indicators, this is an excellent indicator of physician and/or organizational performance.

A productivity-based wRVU contract was put into place for the GBMC physicians to address productivity issues. In the beginning, the majority of the physicians in the LLC were performing below MGMA's 25th percentile in wRVU for similar groups. Today, the majority are at the median level or higher.

The key to productivity and profitability in a practice is how the physicians impact their own revenue. Their behavior is highly correlated to the financial health and cost management of their respective practice.

Physicians react to data. When provided with the relevant data, they can make the decisions. By putting data into useable formats, physicians are allowed to take charge of their practice and productivity.

CHALLENGE

In the beginning, the physician practices were inconsistent in their practice operations, strategic objectives, and priorities. Typically, one question asked would generate several different answers, which is no way to run a successful organization. Further, GBMC's reporting system had no physician-oriented business information system. There were no medical software aids in this reporting to keep track of contract reimbursement, to provide customized information, and to relay any progress physicians and staff achieved.

An organization must have a universally understood set of strategic objectives and priorities. Providing a powerful set of evaluation tools with a virtually limit- less set of data exposes an organization to the whims of individuals willing to manipulate data for their personal agenda. The culture of the physician group lacked "group think," as all the physicians seemed to be out for themselves. Accordingly, tools were put into place to help them understand their roles and align their incentives with that of the organization.

Critical measures had to be instituted to address the lack of a desirable infrastructure and the existing physician culture. To accomplish this goal, GBMC recognized that the organization needed to be properly aligned before initiating these measures.

Accordingly, GBMC administration put together an initiative to educate and communicate what was being watched and measured. Now, the physicians can see how they can earn more. The organization uses a variety of compensation models for the physicians based on productivity, revenue, and operating expenses. The biggest motivator is for physicians to produce more—the more wRVUs they produce the more they take home in income. It can be argued that the physicians are in the business of providing quality care, but, nowhere in this discussion does productivity compromise quality of care.

Operational efficiencies and physician productivity are two key focuses of the group and were vital in moving a medical group to a productivity-based compensation plan with an eye toward cost management. Dashboard reports measured a number of key metrics, many of which were tied to wRVU measurement as compared to MGMA Cost Survey Reports. Physicians and lay staff could understand the organization's and respective physician's data relative to benchmarks. The wRVU is the *gold standard* for measuring data. It is the most accurate methodology for interpreting operating results regarding the practice and analyzing physician wRVU productivity and practice overhead.

The GBMC organization emphasizes productivity and cost-management issues. Using MGMA and regional figures, the administration was able to keep the investment per employed physician in line with MGMA benchmarks even in the face of growth and other investment costs.

INNOVATION

Twaddle uses an assorted page dashboard to show financial and performance comparisons between each provider and MGMA benchmarks. The physicians have their own individual profit centers and receive a second dashboard showing individual performance, which leads to discussions on improvements. Objectives of the dashboards include:

- Allowing the organization to communicate strategies by focusing on metrics enabling physicians and lay staff to understand how well the respective physician's department and the organization are doing;
- Providing timely communication of information allowing for necessary actions to be initiated; and
- Assisting the physicians and lay staff to focus on critical strategic areas by tailoring the dashboard.

Those metric benchmarks are included in two key monthly reports: 1) Physician Profile, and 2) Financial Operational Statistical Analysis (FOSA) report.

PHYSICIAN PROFILE

This monthly report tells physicians everything they need to know about their respective practices. See Figure 9-1 Physician Profile, below, and Figure 9-2,

FIGURE 9-1   Physician Profile

Greater Baltimore Medical Associates   6/10/09[1]
0000000   MEDICINE

	Prior Year /	Average	July	August	Sept	October	November
Target RVU:							
Actual RVU:	5,202	434	306	276	466	542	412
New Pats	96	8	5	3	7	4	4
Encounters	4,712	393	274	228	380	404	326
Level 1	5	0	3	1	10	2	16
Level 2	126	11	5	4	6	2	6
Level 3	3,104	259	197	130	205	230	193
Level 4	1,241	103	68	82	157	150	111
Level 5	6	1	1	1	1	2	1
Other	230	19	4	12	8	21	15
Charges	$551,926	$45,994	$32,705	$28,937	$46,623	$67,657	$49,379
Payments	$(347,517)	$(28,960)	($23,842)	($23,500)	($19,106)	($29,594)	($40,263)
Adjs	$(202,952)	$(16,913)	($16,322)	($13,991)	($10,590)	($15,839)	($25,296)
Ar Bal	$53,851	$53,122	$46,392	$37,838	$54,765	$76,989	$60,808
Days In AR	35.6	35.0	36.1	32.0	46.0	48.9	33.8
Collection %	63.1%	63.1%	59.4%	62.7%	64.3%	65.1%	61.4%

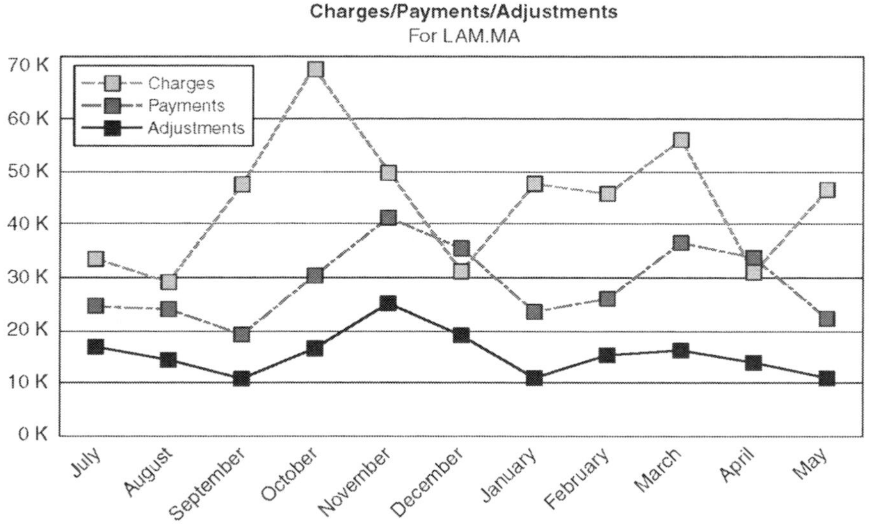

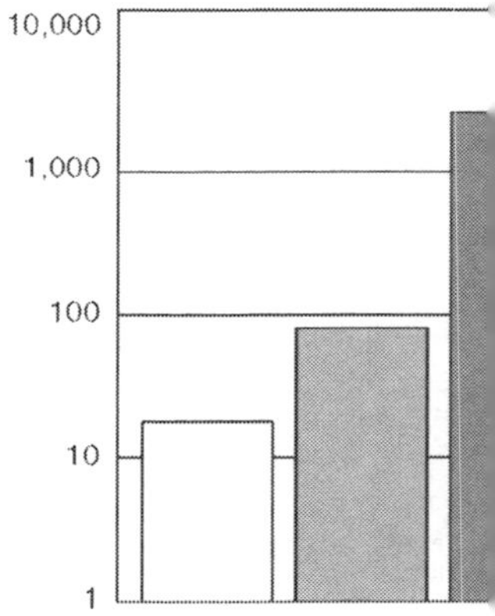

Charges/Payments/Adjustments
For LAM.MA

[1] Reviewed in 2013, this information from 2009 is still relevant for use as an example for educational purposes.

December	January	February	March	April	May	June	YTD
282	378	448	286	446			4,373
1	4	7	11	1	3		50
252	309	381	426	241	352		3,573
2	4	12	8	14	11		74
172	177	233	222	122	181		2,062
72	123	120	153	88	140		1,264
1	1	8					
5	3	15	32	14	20		149
$30,794	$46,569	$44,706	$54,701	$30,250	$45,724	$0	$478,045
($34,360)	($23,122)	($24,639)	($34,930)	($32,835)	($21,201)	$0	$(307,392)
($18,902)	($10,684)	($15,704)	($16,119)	($13,872)	($10,500)	$0	($167,819)
$38,341	$51,104	$55,467	$59,119	$42,662	$56,685	$0	$56,685
23.6	36.7	41.3	36.9	29.9	39.5	-	39.5
64.5%	68.4%	61.1%	68.4%	70.3%	66.9%	-	64.7%

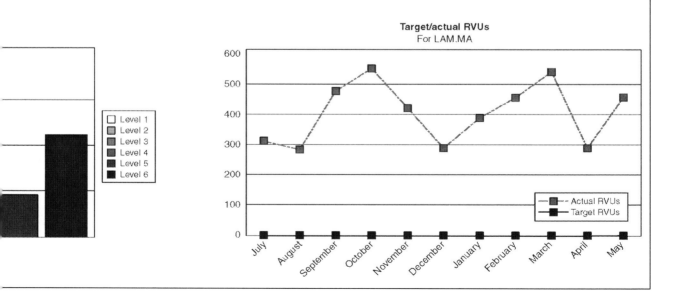

Level 1
Level 2
Level 3
Level 4
Level 5
Level 6

Target/actual RVUs
For LAM.MA

Actual RVUs
Target RVUs

FIGURE 9-2   Physician Profile Reference Sheet for Definitions and Explanations

Work-Only Component of Relative Value Units (wRVUs)
Unit of measure of physician work. Relative value units assigned to each procedure or service reflect physician work, defined as time, mental effort and judgment, technical skill, physician effort, and stress involved in delivering care.[1]

Target
wRVU value determined by physician representative of level of effort desires to achieve each month. There is a direct correlation to physician's wRVU contract.

Actual RVU
Actual count of wRVUs as compiled by the hospital Practice Management System based on the volumes and appropriate assignment of visit levels and procedures provided by the physician during the time period.

New Patient
A new patient is one who has not received any professional services within the past three years from the physician or any physician of the same specialty who belongs to the same group practice.[2] An increasing number of new patients would indicate the practice is growing.

Total Encounters
An encounter is defined as documented face-to-face contact between a patient and a provider who exercises independent judgment in the provision of patient services. Two visits during the same day with the same diagnosis are counted by the hospital Practice Management System as one encounter.

Level 1 through Level 5 and Other Encounters
Subcategories of evaluation and management (E&M) services are further divided into levels of E&M services that are identified by specific codes. Table 9-1 below identifies by current procedural terminology (CPT) code the level or other category assigned for each level.

Charges
Charges are defined as the total gross billed charges by the provider to the patient or third-party payer before any discount or adjustment. Charges are compiled by the Practice Management System based on the volume and appropriate management of visit levels and procedures extended by the respective unit price. The accounts receivable balance increases as charges are posted in the system.

Payments
Payments are received, deposited, and posted (recorded) in the Practice Management System. As the payments are received, the accounts receivable balance is reduced. This line reflects payments toward active accounts receivable. Certain other payments, including capitation payments and bad debt recoveries, are not reflected here.

Adjustments
All other transactions affecting the active accounts receivable balance except charges and payments are recorded as adjustments. Normal adjustments reduce accounts receivable and include contractual adjustments, from governmental and nongovernmental payers, courtesy adjustments, charity adjustments, other adjustments, and transferred balances to bad debts. The Practice Management System compiles these transactions and reports these activities for the period.

Accounts Receivable Balance
This balance is maintained by the Practice Management System and represents gross amounts outstanding. Notice the new balance at the end of the current month is the sum of the balance at the end of the previous months minus net payments minus net adjustments for the current month.

Days in Accounts Receivable
This amount is calculated and provides an indication of how many days on average after the service is provided until the cash is collected. Using the charge information, an average daily charge is first calculated. The accounts receivable balance is then divided by the average daily charge to arrive at how many days of gross revenue is outstanding in the accounts receivable balance. A lower number is desired.

[1] *RBRV Fee Schedule: A Plain English Guide, 2007 Edition. Rockville, MD: Decision Health p. 77.*
[2] *CPT 2007, Chicago, IL: American Medical Association, p. 1.*

FIGURE 9-2   Physician Profile Reference Sheet for Definitions and Explanations   *(Continued)*

Collection Percentage
This amount is calculated and provides an indication of the percentage of gross charges that are actually being collected after all adjustments are recorded including transfers to bad debt. The calculation divides the payments (cash collections), the sum of the payments, and adjustments for the period.

TABLE 9-1   Physician Profile Mapping

Encounters	Level 1	Level 2	Level 3	Level 4	Level 5	Other	New Patients
Office—New	99201 thru 99205	99201	99202	99203	99204	99205	
Office—Established	99211 thru 99215	99211	99212	99213	99214	99215	
Inpatient—Initial	99221 thru 99223	99221	99222	99223			
Inpatient—Subsequent	99231 thru 99233	99231	99232	99233			
Inpatient—Discharge	99238 thru 99239						
Observe—Initial	99218 thru 99220	99218	99219	99220			
Observe—Subsequent	99234 thru 99236	99234	99235	99236			
Observe—Discharge	99217						
Consults, Office	99241 thru 99245	99241	99242	99243	99244	99245	
Consults, Inpatient	99251 thru 99255	99251	99252	99253	99254	99255	
Emergency Department	99281 thru 99285	99281	99281	99283	99281	99285	
Nsg Home—Initial	99304 thru 99306	99304	99305	99306			
Nsg Home—Subsequent	99307 thru 99310	99307	99308	99309	99310		
Nsg Home—Discharge	99315 thru 99316						
Nsg—Annual	99318						
Opthalmology—New	92002 thru 92004	92002	62004	92002-04			
Opthalmology—Established	92012 thru 92014	99212	92014				
Prevent—New	99381 thru 99387						
Prevent—Established	99391 thru 99397						
Prevent—Counsel	99401 thru 99404						
Newborn	99431 thru 99433						
Newborn	99435 thru 99436						
Newborn	99440						
Critical Care	99291 thru 99296						
Critical Care	99298 thru 99300						
Obstetrics	59425 thru 59426						
Obstetrics	59430						

Physician Profile Reference Sheet for Definitions and Explanations to gain a better understanding of this report, including wRVUs, charges, payments, level of coding, encounters, accounts receivable, and days in accounts receivable). The physician knows firsthand how the practice is performing. This is especially important since this same document drives the compensation for physicians participating in a wRVU-type contract. Many of the physicians will monitor their own data and compare those data to this report. Variances typically deal with payer denials and those CPT-4 codes not having assigned wRVU values. More discussion follows on how to address CPT-4 codes without wRVU values.

Compliance issues are always foremost in our minds. The following section addresses the calculation of an acuity ratio calculated from physicians' wRVU production as seen in their representative Physician Profile.

Level of Coding

Evaluation and management (E&M) codes, the most commonly billed codes, are applied to primary care, subspecialty, and surgery practices. Services billed to either the Centers for Medicare & Medicaid Services (CMS) or commercial carriers are usually defined by the code descriptor while the various E&M codes rely on the physician's judgment of the medical necessity for the service.

Let's put the value of a bell curve in proper perspective (see Figure 9-1, Physician Profile) when reviewing E&M codes. The statistics of physician code usage reflected in the report can be useful for evaluating an individual's coding patterns. However, when a physician's code usage, "care level," is outside the bell curve, one should not assume that this represents fraudulent coding. Typically, usage patterns are unique to each specialty. Numerous benchmark data are available from CMS; Decision Health, a commercial firm specializing in compliance data; or even by comparing peers within a medical group. While there are regional differences, CMS and the U.S. Department of Health and Human Services Office of Inspector General use similar databases to screen coding outliers.

The "care levels," or acuity, can be seen easily in the bar chart. There are five care levels detailed in this report. Each is representative of the level of care provided each patient and has a corresponding wRVU assigned to it. As mentioned earlier, the grouping of CPT-4 codes within each care level are summarized in Table 9-1, Physician Profile Mapping.

Acuity

Acuity (Table 9-2), represented in the Physician Profile, is designed to measure the consumption of resources for a specific procedure or service, in patient care, over a set period of time. The more complex the procedure or service, the greater the overall complexity of services being provided, and the higher the wRVU values. In essence, this is the ratio of wRVUs for each procedure or service pro- vided. Acuity can be calculated simply as shown below:

Acuity = (Total No. of wRVU Billed) / (Total No. of Encounters Billed)

TABLE 9-2 Acuity			
	Prior Year Current (YTD)	Annualized Variance	Percentage
Actual wRVU	4,275	5,203	
Encounters	7,376	4,937	
Acuity Ratio	.580	1.054	+81.7

The acuity levels can be trended. They can be compared to national or peer statistics within the department to indicate whether the coding is to the left or right of the national or peer bell curve. In the example shown in Table 9-2, prior year acuity ratio is shown to be .580 while current YTD trending is 1.054, indicating a significant change of coding activity, (+81.7 percent), has occurred over the prior period.

Other data need to be reviewed when a physician's coding pattern seems aberrant. If possible, generate a report from your practice management system reflecting the diagnosis codes that have been billed for all of the E&M codes. If these diagnoses are for chronic conditions, it is likely the services are medically necessary and, if well-documented, are coded correctly. However, if a portion of the E&M visits are linked to diagnosis codes that you would not usually expect to require a high level of service, these records should be reviewed for medical necessity and documentation.

This is usually the focus of an insurance payer profiling exercise. When a physician has a higher cost, in this case a higher acuity ratio than his or her peers, the payer may be prompted to compare the physician's CPT-4 code usage in an attempt to evaluate whether the service provided appears appropriate.

FOSA

The FOSA report pulls together a number of key elements found in the hospital's accounting, accounts payable, and payroll systems, which all tie into the hospital reporting system. The report is constructed to be matched against MGMA benchmarks. This report was pulled together because there was no business intelligence system and is a composite of multiple financial, accounting, and payroll systems, which were designed to combine one reporting system.

The result was a four-part report that concentrates on the following groupings: 1) Operating Statement; 2) Volume Indicators; 3) Expense Indicators; and 4) Statistical Data. Table 9-3, FOSA Summary Report Sections, identifies key elements, including wRVU components, which can be measured against benchmark data.

Using the FOSA data will assist each of GBMCs 41 practice managers for a number of reasons. They include:

- Practice managers will better understand the difference between their practice and others within their respective system and/or compared to MGMA's Cost Survey benchmarks.

- If there are variances, practice managers can determine if they indicate a significant variance requiring practice manager intervention?
- Interpreting the data is critical. It is important to understand any variances and how the data were compiled. Many variances occur as a result of internal accounting coding errors. Just knowing the source of data within the FOSA report and how they compared to MGMA's Cost Survey data will help the practice managers focus on problem areas.
- The data will reveal whether the variances are a result of internal or external factors and whether they can be controlled or changed.
- Practice managers can better determine what weight the variances have on the performance of the organization as a whole? Significant variances might require additional leadership support.

ASSIGNMENT OF WRVU TO NON-CPT-4 CODES

As discussed in prior chapters, CMS and the RVS Update Committee (RUC), working together, establish the wRVUs. Practices typically provide some services within their office that are not necessarily found under CMS CPT-4 terminology. Accordingly, no assigned wRVUs are applied to these codes. Categories of services you would find in these areas include: 1) nonstandard codes, 2) teaching, and 3) directorships for services outside of clinical practices. Organizations would have to define the services and come up with a methodology to determine the value. Different criteria include time and effort of service, costs associated with the service, and/or, comparative code analysis.

Nonstandard CPT-4 Codes

Resource-based relative value scales (RBRVSs) are used to assign wRVUs to CPT-4 procedures. The most current values should be used to update wRVUs annually. Of those codes that do not have wRVUs, some do have practice expense and malpractice units assigned. See Figure 9-3, Methodology Used to Assign wRVUs for CPT-4 codes and GBMC codes that do not have assigned wRVUs values. For other codes, there are no units assigned for work, practice expense, or malpractice. Table 9-4, as shown within Figure 9-3, shows an assigned RVUs extract.

Teaching Relative Value Units

Teaching relative value units for Internal Medicine faculty teaching activities are another derivative. It is important to track faculty teaching RVUs because of the volume of nonclinical time and productivity expected of Internal Medicine instructors. Doing so will place value on nonclinical time and productivity and offer incentives for teaching, administration, scholarship, and quality. Teaching RVUs will provide metrics for monitoring scholarly activities essential for accreditation and improve institutional decision making regarding the clinic. This is critical in order to achieve a balance between the practice and scholarly activities.

TABLE 9-3 FOSA SUMMARY	
Cost Centers	999999
Description	Dr. Health
Specialty	Fam Prac
Location	PPE
Solo/Group	Solo
Section 1	
Operating Statement:	Example
Revenues	
Medicare	$45,100
Medicaid	$7,602
Blue Cross	$34,686
Commercial	$18,136
HMO	$8,410
Self Pay	$1,925
Workman Comp	$170
Other	$1,134
Capitation	$1,934
	$119,097
Total Part B - Revenue	$119,097
Part B - Allowances	($34,605)
Bad Debt	($5,222)
Net Revenue (Part B)	$79,271
Net Revenue (Part A)	$-
Other Operating Revenue	$-
Total Revenue	$79,271
Expenses	
Salaries w/o Drs. Payment	$22,754
Physician Incentives	$4,866
Physician Salaries	$19,680
Physician Draw	$11,538
Contracted Physicians	$-
FICA	($1,114)
Other Benefits	$-
Expendable Supplies	$2,800

(Continued)

TABLE 9-3   FOSA SUMMARY   *(Continued)*

Insurances	$2,274
Billing Fees	$6,954
Office Space Rental	$6,173
Other Purchased Services	$2,930
Depreciation	$-
Interest	$-
Overhead	$-
Total Expenses	$78,855
Operating Income/Loss	$416
Section 2 Indicators	
Volume Indicators:	Example
RVU/Clinical FTE	1,231.85
Encounter/Clinical FTE	616
Target Encounter/Clinical FTE	na
Gross Revenue/Clinical FTE	$119,097
Net Revenue/Clinical FTE	$79,271
Payer Mix Indicators:	
Revenue by payer:	
Medicare	37.87%
Medicaid	6.38%
Blue Cross	29.12%
Commercial	15.23%
HMO	7.06%
Self Pay	1.62%
Workman Comp	0.14%
Other	0.95%
Capitation	1.62%
	100.00%
Pricing Indicators:	
Gross Revenue/RVU	$96.68
Gross Revenue/Encounter	$193.34
Collection Indicators:	
Net Revenue/Gross Billing	66.60%
Uncollectable Portion	33.40%

(Continued)

TABLE 9-3 FOSA SUMMARY *(Continued)*	
Section 3 Indicators	
Expense Indicators:	Example
Expense/Revenue:	
Salaries w/o Drs. Payment	28.70%
Physician Incentives	6.14%
Physician Salary & Draw	39.38%
Contracted Physicians	0.00%
FICA	-1.41%
Other Benefits	0.00%
Expendable Supplies	3.53%
Insurances	2.87%
Billing Fees	8.77%
Office Space Rental	7.79%
Other Purchased Services	3.70%
Depreciation	0.00%
Interest	0.00%
Overhead	0.00%
Total Expenses	99.48%
Operating Income/Loss	0.52%
Staff FTE/Clinical FTE	3.15
Staff Sal.Exp./Clinical FTE	$22,754
Supplies Expense/RVU	$2.27
Insurance Exp./Clinical FTE	$2,274
Billing fees % of Collection	8.70%
Sq. Ft./Clinical FTE	1,390.00
Office Rental/sq. foot	$4
Office Rental/Clinical FTE	$6,173
All Non-Sal. Exp./Clinical FTE	$20,017
Provider Comp./Clinical FTE	$36,084
Total Expense/Clinical FTE	$78,855
Total Expense/Clinical FTE (calc)	$78,855
Accounts Receivable:	
Gross Days in AR	32.27
Net Days in AR	28.11

(Continued)

TABLE 9-3 FOSA SUMMARY *(Continued)*	
Section 4	
Stastical Data:	Example
RVU per Profile	1,232
Encounters per Profile	616
Target Encounters	
Provider Compensation	36,084
Provider Headcount	1
Provider FTE	1
Clinical FTE	1
Staff FTE	3.15
Total FTE	4.15
Total FTE-Calc	4.15
Square Footage	1,390
Beginning Gross AR	74,150
Charges	116,114
Payments	-79,883
Adustments	-48,388
Ending Gross-AR	61,993
Ending Gross-AR-Calc	61,993
Beginning Net AR	52,937
Increase in Net AR	-16,992
Ending Net AR	35,945
Ending Net AR-Calc	35,945
Net Revenue-Calc	64,825

Why is scholarship important? The Accreditation Council for Graduate Medical Education (ACGME) requires that faculty participate in scholarly activities. This requirement is clearly defined in the program requirements for residency education in internal medicine. Hospitals are normally cited for not showing sufficient support for scholarship.

Many programs provide an academic incentive allocated using the following formula:

(Individual Teaching RVUs / Group TVUs achieved) X Total Allocated
Incentive Dollars = Allocated TVU Dollars.

This easily can be broken down into teaching, scholarship, administrative, and quality categories. Academic institutions that use a variation of the Teaching

FIGURE 9-3   Methodology for Assigning Work wRVUs

Different methodologies are used for arriving at the wRVUs for CPT codes and GBMA codes that do not have assigned wRVUs. Samples of these methodologies are outlined and numbered below. Each code shown in Table 9-4, Assigned RVUs Extract, has a corresponding methodology number given.

TABLE 9-4   Assigned RVUs Extract

Group	Procedure	Description	Work RVU	Comperative Code	Total RVUs	M	Comments
MD	1	Copying Medical Records	0.09	99211	0	2	Assume this requires a degree of physicians over-site, but typically not as much as nurse visit. Allowed 50% of work RVU for 99211.
MD	2	Completing Insurance Form	0.07	99211	0	2	Assume physician completes the disability form personally
MD	20930	Allograft for spine surgery	1	20931	0	4	Morselized bone graft carries no RVUs. Structural bone graft carries 1.81 work RVU.
MD	99455	Disability Examination	0.67	99213	0	2	Compared to 99213

For codes that already have a wRVU value assigned on the RBRVS, the actual wRVU value for that code is used.

For services that are typically provided in a practice but do not have a CPT-4 code, or have a CPT-4 code for which there are no work units assigned (such as copying records, disability exams, etc.) these services are compared to E&M codes times and have the referenced CPTs code listed in the comparative code column.

For those services that are part of global services, no work units are assigned. RVUs are assigned to the global code. (This includes prenatal visits and postoperative visits). For those codes that are procedural in scope and have no work units assigned (temporary codes, unlisted codes, etc.) we attempt to find similar services with a wRVU value. The performing physician is consulted before wRVUs are finalized.

For surgery codes with an -80, AS, or -50 modifier, wRVUs are assigned as follows:
-80 = 16 percent of the surgery RVUs for assistant at surgery,
AS = 16 percent of the surgery RVUs for assistant at surgery,
-50 = Twice the wRVUs for bilateral procedures.

For those codes that have -0- work units assigned and do not represent additional work for the physician, no wRVUs are assigned.

When total RVUs are available and the total RVU is small (under 1.00) we allotted 50 percent of the total RVUs to work.

On the accompanying spreadsheet, the columns provide the following information:

G	Group: The codes are divided into two groups.
MD	Services typically provided by a physician
A	Services typically provided by ancillary staff
Procedure	Internal or CPT-4 procedure
Description	The internal description of the code
Work RVU	wRVUs assigned based on explained methodology
Comparative code	CPT-4 code used to arrive at recommended RVU
Total RVUs	Total RVUs is given if the CPT code had no work RVUs but was assigned PE and Malpractice RVUs
M	Methodology used to assign RVU
Comments	An explanation of the methodology used for the code addressed

RVUs system include University of Pittsburgh, University of Kentucky, and Louisiana State University. They have proposed Teaching RVUs equal the hours assigned to the activity multiplied by the dollar relative value factor (RVF). RVF value depends on the activities' ability to impact the educational mission, national recognition, recruitment, and marketing of the organization.

Geriatrics Value Units (GVUs) for Directorship

This specialty faces similar conditions as Internal Medicine. It is not uncommon for a physician in this specialty to receive directorship funding for services performed in a nursing home. Combined with mid-level services, a pool of monies is available for distribution based on a weighted wRVU allocation method.

GVU, a pseudo-wRVU, would have to be calculated similarly to a Teaching RVU, mentioned above, to incorporate monies received from nursing homes with that of the clinical practices. It is important to factor operating costs before determining dollar conversion rate. There has been much deliberation over the most appropriate manner in which to allocate these fundings, but this method has been found to be one of the fairest methods for all parties.

It has been proposed that GVU equals hours assigned to the activity multiplied by dollar RVF. The RVF value must consider direct and indirect overhead expenses in this calculation.

ICD-10 and RVUs

October 1, 2014 is the planned implementation date for ICD-10 Clinical Modification (CM) and ICD-10 Procedure Coding System (PCS). Though the goals of utilizing ICD-10 are to provide greater details of diagnoses and improve the description of work being performed, implementation will likely cause significant disruption to physician productivity at a high implementation expense.

Virtually every business aspect of a practice will be impacted by ICD-10 implementation with significant expense incurred for staffing, training, and billing mainly due to decreased production at all levels in the practice. Though the billing and coding staff may require extended training on billing and filing claims appropriately with this new code set, none will be impacted more profoundly than the physicians and clinical staff that must ensure the documentation supports the level of service billed.

The need for specificity in documentation will increase significantly as the number of diagnosis codes increases from 14,000 to more than 69,000 codes. Physicians will require intense training to teach them documentation details that must be included such as laterality, stages of healing, weeks in pregnancy, episodes of care, etc. This increased documentation could result in decreased production, translating to decreased wRVUs. Careful planning and implementation strategies are required to budget for cash flow disruptions coupled with decreased production.

Accountable Care Organizations

Accountable care organizations (ACOs) are being established across the nation in the form of Medicare or commercial ACOs with a large portion being physician-led. If the goal is to reduce the cost of healthcare in the United States, physician compensation models must also be aligned with incentives for ACOs. Accordingly, productivity must include measures other than clinical productivity. Complementing a wRVU incentive model with qualitative measures such as patient satisfaction, mortality, and morbidity or other outcome metrics will bridge the gap while transitioning toward more evidence-based medicine and the anticipated "value based modifier" for Medicare patients coming in 2015. ACOs will need physicians to lead in the operations, innovation, quality, and customer service areas, and in particular, patient-centered medical home care management. Metrics easily can be assigned to each of these activities along with a nonstandard CPT-4 code when calculating productivity.

CONCLUSION

Twaddle emphasizes, "New goals in wRVU and cost management will continue to be set for years to come. Providing the necessary data for physicians to manage is paramount to the success of the organization. It is now the culture of the group. As long as we do this, I think we can continue to grow."

10

The Future of RVUs

Relative value units (RVUs) are used robustly in medical practice now, but how will they be used in the future? This chapter takes a look ahead at RVUs and their derivatives and offer some insight into potential uses and what to expect down the road.

First, it is safe to say that RVUs have had a sufficiently significant impact on the medical profession to conclude that they are here for the long term. One reason is the disparity in reimbursement, but even in the case of a single-payer system in the United States, RVUs would still be a valuable management tool. That tool would require certain enhancements to respond to whatever form of reimbursement system were in existence. Even in the "accountable care era" (as we discuss in Chapter 9) RVUs have a place in our performance evaluation measurements. Yes, RVUs are here to stay.

There are other possibilities for expanding the utilization of RVUs. For example, the structure of RVUs could change if the system transcends to a payment structure that bundles structural practice components or a bundled coordination component that recognizes the work value of the physician and nonphysician clinical and administrative care coordination activities that occur outside the patient encounter. In addition, in moving toward a performance-based component that recognizes achievement of quality and efficiency goals, the RVU process may need to change. Hospitals and physician reimbursement may one day be combined. Such a dramatic change would require a significant overhaul of the current resource-based relative value scale (RBRVS), and ultimately the RVU derivatives. Nonetheless, with such new features in place (even in a fee-for-value setting), RVUs can be a means to tabulate, aggregate, and measure performance.

This chapter will delve briefly into some of these possibilities. First to con- sider is the current process for updating the relative value scale on a regular basis through a defined process of the RVS Update Committee (RUC). However, keep in mind in the discussion of possibilities for the future that there are no certainties and tremendous unknowns.

RVS UPDATE COMMITTEE AND ITS PROCESS

When Medicare moved toward a physician payment system based on RBRVS, the American Medical Association sensed that changes would need to be made on a regular basis to the individual unit values. Thus, it created the RUC, which has presented significant change recommendations to the Centers for Medicare & Medicaid Services (CMS) recently. In turn, many of these significant changes that were recommended have been adopted by CMS. At times, these have resulted in some rather dramatic adjustments to RVU values. Nonetheless, the RUC has provided physicians a voice in shaping the relative values.

The RUC, in conjunction with the CPT Editorial Panel, established a process whereby specific specialties can submit recommendations for new code values. They can also make recommendations for new codes in and of themselves. The RUC assumes the responsibility of analysis of these requests and formulates recommendations to CMS for adoption.

Historical examples of such accomplishments include:

- *January 1997.* This was the first five-year review process, which established a precedent of a much more detailed process of reviewing practice expense and the work-only component of relative-value units (wRVUs) compared to the entire Medicare relative value scale. As a result of the January 1997 RUC review, it submitted more than 1,000 current procedural terminology (CPT) codes that largely entailed increases to the evaluation and management (E&M) codes. While not required to accept these, CMS in fact acknowledged about 95% of the RUC's recommendations. This involved specific changes in RVU values to approximately 400 codes.

- *January 2002.* The second five-year review resulted in the RUC recommending changes to fewer than 900 CPT codes. CMS accepted 98% of the RUC's recommendations.

- *January 2007.* The third five-year RUC review resulted in significant increases to work relative values for E&M services. It should be noted that RVU values are not always increased. In fact, in the January 2007 RUC recommendations, several codes were recommended for decrease. Overall, the standard plan is to maintain RVU values at a relatively neutral point from one update to another.

- *January 2009.* CMS accepted and implemented all of the RUC's recommendations, which resulted after the Committee's Five-Year Review Identification Workgroup aimed at identifying inaccurate physician service values. CMS' decision to use the RUC recommendations yielded in a small increase in the 2009 Medicare Conversion Factor.

- *January 2012.* CMS released the revised codes based on its solicitation of the RUC's comments during its fourth five-year review on over 290 codes identified by specialties. The RUC submitted its comments for CMS' consideration on October 2010 and February 2011. CMS accepted 75% of the RUC's recommendations.

As the "accountable care era" evolves, the RUC's involvement in CMS' medical home pilot becomes increasingly urgent. While the RUC was initially engaged to evaluate reimbursement rates with the medical home initiative in 2008, as of late 2011 and into 2012, it has been a pivotal force in urging CMS to begin compensating for care coordination. Specifically, the committee challenged CMS to prove its commitment to patient-centered medical homes and begin reimbursing for procedures that provide care coordination for the chronically ill, including telephone consults with patients; education and training for patient self-management performed by non-physician care givers; medical team conferences; and anticoagulation management. The RUC's recommendation was intended to promote short-term payments for efforts aimed at cutting unnecessary visits, medications and/or hospitalizations, and ultimately incentivize care delivery reform. Such fee-for-value precepts work well with the existing RVU structure as establishing codes/procedures for care coordination is easily accommodated via the traditional means of valuing the work overhead and professional liability components into an RVU value.

As of August 2012, the RUC submitted its comments on CMS' Notice of Proposed Rule Making (NPRM) on the revisions to Medicare reimbursement policies under the 2013 Physician Payment Schedule. In its letter, the committee offered its recommendations on various CMS topics, including (but not limited to) care coordination services, expanding the Multiple Procedure Payment Reduction Policy, and misvalued codes on the 2013 fee schedule.

The RUC has proven to be a viable entity, respected by CMS, and in a positive way features input from the provider side of reimbursement. Through the reimbursement increase, changes occur through the changes in RVU values, which are the basis of Medicare reimbursements.

RVU UPDATING

While the RUC completes a formal review every five years, annual updates to the physician wRVUs are recommended. Actually formed in 1991, the RUC provides recommendations to CMS on the relative value scales to be assigned to new or revised codes. As such, there are more than 8,600 procedure codes defined in CPT, with the relative values in the RBRVS system developed to correlate to the procedure definitions in CPT.

CPT is maintained by an editorial panel. This 17-member entity is commissioned with the responsibility to revise, update, or modify CPT. Representatives include American Medical Association nominees, those recommended by the Blue Cross and Blue Shield Association, the Health Insurance Association of America (HIAA), CMS, and the American Hospital Association (AHA). Annually the coding system is updated, which would include the addition and deletion of specific codes.

RUC represents the entire medical profession with most of its 29 members appointed by major or national medical specialty societies.

Table 10-1 summarizes the RUC representatives.

TABLE 10-1   Representations of the RUC Committee[1]

Chair
American Medical Association
CPT Editorial Panel
American Osteopathic Association
Health Care Professional Advisory Committee
Practice Expense Subcommittee

Anesthesiology	Obstetrics/Gynecology
Cardiology	Ophthalmology
Cardiothoracic Surgery	Orthopedic Surgery
Dermatology	Otolaryngology
Emergency Medicine	Pathology
Family Medicine	Pediatrics
Gastroenterology*	Pediatric Surgery*
General Surgery	Plastic Surgery
Infectious Disease*	Psychiatry
Internal Medicine	Radiology
Neurology	Urology
Neurosurgery	

(*Indicates rotating seat)

Advisory Committee

One physician representative is appointed from each of the 109 specialty societies seated in the AMA House of Delegates to serve on the *Advisory Committee* to the RUC. Specialty societies that are not in the House of Delegates also may be invited to participate in developing relative values for coding changes of particular relevance to their members. Advisory committee members designate an *RVS Committee* for their specialty, which is responsible for generating relative value recommendations using a survey method developed by the RUY. The Advisors attend the RUC meeting and present their societies' recommendations, which the RUC evaluates. Specialties represented on both the RUC and the Advisory Committee are required to appoint different physicians to each committee to distinguish the role of advocate from that of evaluator.

[1]American Medical Association (AMA)/Specialty Society; *RYS Update Process.* http://www.ama-assn.org/ama1/pub/uploadhnm/380/rvsbooklet 07.pdf. Accessed August 22, 2009.

The RUC process for developing relative value recommendations follows a specific eight-step process, as outlined in Table 10-2. The following information is based on a position paper published by the American Medical Association.[2]

FUTURE REIMBURSEMENT STRUCTURES

RVUs as a measure of productivity affect reimbursement significantly, especially within governmental forms of third-party payer relationships such as Medicare and Medicaid. In the healthcare industry's attempt to respond to economic pressures and demands for healthcare in the United States, the delivery and payment system will consider significant changes that may soon go into effect.

---

[2] AMA/Specialty Society. *RVS Update Process.* American Medical Association. Accessed on June 18, 2009. Available at http://www.ama-assn.org/ama1/pub/upload/mm/380/rvs_booklet_07.pdf.

TABLE 10-2 RUC Process for Developing Relative Value Recommendations	
Step 1	CPT Editorial Panel's new or revised codes are transmitted to RUC staff. RUC staff prepares a "level of interest" form.
Step 2	Members of the RUC Advisory Committee and specialty society staff review the summary, and then indicate their societies' level of interest in developing relative value recommendations. Options include:
1.	Survey members to obtain data on amount of work involved in a service, to develop recommendations based on their survey results.
2.	Comment in writing on recommendations developed by other societies.
3.	For revised codes, decide that the coding change does not require action due to an insignificant change in the nature of the service.
4.	Take no action in that codes are not used by physicians in their specialty.
Step 3	American Medical Association staff distributes survey instruments for specialty societies. Societies must survey at least 30 practicing physicians. Physicians receiving surveys must evaluate the work involved in the new or revised code relative to certain reference points.
Step 4	Specialty Relative Value Scale (RVS) committees conduct surveys for their specialty, review results, and compile recommendations to the RUC. Written recommendations are disseminated to the RUC prior to its meeting.
Step 5	Specialty advisors present recommendations to the RUC. Question and answer period follows.
Step 6	The RUC may respond in one of three ways:
1.	Adopt a specialty society's recommendation.
2.	Refer the recommendation back to the specialty society.
3.	Modify the recommendation before submitting to CMS.
	Final recommendations to CMS require a two-thirds majority of the RUC members.
Step 7	RUC's recommendations are forwarded to CMS in May of each year. CMS medical officers and contractor medical directors review the RUC's recommendations.
Step 8	The Medicare Physician Payment Schedule, which includes CMS's review of the RUC recommendations, is published by the late fall of each year.

The trend of healthcare delivery and payment system for the future appears to be toward a multicomponent bundled payment structure that, at least in theory, provides more effective and efficient care delivery for patients. In most instances, strategists are suggesting that this be done through the advanced medical home (AMH). AMH is a care delivery model that (again, in theory) offers the advantages of a personal physician, but does this within a provider system that accepts overall responsibility for the care of the patient, with a team approach, providing enhanced access to care. Coordination and integration of care, with emphasis on safety and quality, are also a part of the AMH.

Corresponding with the AMH, a new risk-adjusted payment structure has been proposed, as outlined in the American College of Physicians' Position Paper, as follows.[3]

[3] American College of Physicians. *A System in Need of Change: Restructuring Payment Policies to Support Patient-Centered Care. Position Paper.* Philadelphia: American College of Physicians, 2006. Available from American College of Physicians, 190 N. Independence Mall West, Philadelphia, PA 19106.

- *A prospective bundled structural practice component.* This would offset overhead of the practice tied to the provision of AMH services not currently paid under the present system.
- *A prospective bundled care coordination component.* This would recognize the work value of the physician (analogous to a wRVU) plus the nonphysician clinical and administrative care coordination functions that occur outside of actual encounter visits (again, not currently paid under the present system).
- *An encounter-based fee-for-service component.* This would consider visit-based services that are a part of the current reimbursement system.
- *A performance-based component.* This would recognize the attainment of quality and efficiency standards within the patient encounter process.

Other components that likely will be a part of any new payment system would be the inclusion of implementation of health information technology (HIT) and performance reporting through incentive provisions.

In addition, many (including the American College of Physicians in the above-noted report) are calling for the termination of the Medicare sustainable growth rate (SGR) formula, which has heretofore been the basis for physician fee changes from year to year. A transitional pathway to accomplish this process that would ultimately result in a more predictable methodology for updating physician payment reimbursement while still emphasizing high-quality cost effective care is recommended as an alternative. As such, the American College of Physicians has suggested that a new methodology for establishing the annual Medicare fee schedule payment updates should be based on an annual Medicare Payment Advisory Commission (MedPAC). Key components within this revised payment schedule include the following:

- A stable percentage update (also specified to be a positive percentage each year) in the Medicare conversion factor applicable to all services. This would take into account all cost of delivery of care, beneficiary access to services, the cost of the workforce, and other data that may affect access and quality.
- Another percentage amount above the Medicare baseline spending for physician services to fund a physician's quality improvement pool.
- Optional targeted "add-ons" for payments regarding a certain category of services designed to respond to the achievement of policy objectives.

The drivers of such dramatic changes in the current reimbursement structure are the reality of healthcare costs growing faster than the economy, and the cost of care becoming increasingly more challenging for various components of our society to support, including employers, individuals, and the government. Employers are seeking ways to cut back on the benefits they provide—not only for their current employee base, but for retiree benefits, as well. Concurrently, insurance premiums from third-party insurers are increasing at record rates. In addition, some believe there are significant gaps in the quality of healthcare that is provided in the United States. They support this premise by stating that outcomes vary dramatically despite efforts to the contrary. Many users of healthcare, the patients, are dissatisfied with the care they receive, and, in particular, they dissatisfied with their providers—both physicians and hospitals. Finally, the physicians providing care—from the primary care providers to the specialists—are becoming increasingly dissatisfied with the way they are asked to practice medicine, especially considering the financial and administrative demands and stresses placed on them.

Thus, the current healthcare system's challenges may indeed force some or all of the changes noted. By all accounts, the major shortage in primary care physicians has warranted a medical workforce crisis nationwide, with rural areas being affected significantly more than their urban counterparts.[4] Despite federal and private efforts toward primary care development, the number of new physicians entering into primary care is continuing to go down as many physicians opt to become specialists simply because of the dramatic differences in their income earning ability.[5] When this dramatic difference is extrapolated over an entire career, the income-earning potential of a specialist easily can be two to three times that of the primary care physician.[6]

The emerged accountable care era has brought forth several care delivery structures that represent the new wave of reimbursement. Under this umbrella we have the accountable care organization (ACO), clinically integrated network/organization (CIN/CIO), as well as the PCMH and AMH. A prominent feature of all of these systems is the creation of value on which a portion of their reimbursement will rely (i.e., giving rise to fee-for-value).

All of these models are geared toward achieving population health management through the delivery of high-quality, patient-centric, and cost-effective care. These structures all depend on clinical integration and a robust information technology infrastructure. Through the appropriate use of integration, IT, evidence-based medicine, as well as appropriate alignment of incentives among all participants, a major goal of the accountable care era structures is to realize significant cost savings. The underlying concept behind this theory (which has been proven on several accounts, i.e., Geisinger Health System, Intermountain Health System, etc.) is as quality of care increases and unnecessary services are eliminated, cost savings are achieved and greater revenue is generated. It is through the achievement of savings that these models remain sustainable and providers remain engaged, in that the savings are not only compensating them for their services, but also holding them accountable for their performance.

[4] Bodenheimer, T., Pham, H. H. (2010). Primary Care: Current Problems and Proposed Solutions. *Health Affairs*, 29(5), 799-805.
[5] Cooney, Elizabeth, "Pay gap widens between primary care doctors, specialists," White Coat Notes. Accessed 9/24/2009. Available at http://www.boston.com/yourlife/health/blog/2007/02/ pay_gap_widens.html.
[6] "Primary Care Medicine—Undervalued in America," The Society for Patient Centered Orthopedics. Accessed 9/24/2009. Available at http://www.thepatientfirst.org/rescuing-primary-care- and-fixing-our-system.html.

Accountable Care Organizations:

The primary focus of an ACO is to reduce hospital admissions and/or length of stay, reduce emergency room visits, and improve quality of care. Most ACOs are CMS-based and as such, accept only Medicare beneficiaries. For the participating providers, Medicare reimbursements will make up the majority of their compensation, with standard fee-for-service reimbursement and also payments relying on several key metrics assessing quality. Herein lies the "accountability" factor within an ACO.

In a shared savings program, the ACO is charged with controlling costs while still providing quality care. Quality, in this case, will be determined by several predetermined metrics such as readmission rates and patient outcomes. Providers can share the savings amongst themselves, use it to reinvest in the ACO infrastructure, or do both. Additionally, if a certain level of cost reduction (or quality) is not achieved, the ACO will be responsible for paying Medicare a certain amount. Thus, this model is based on financial incentives and penalties.

Clinically Integrated Networks/Organizations:

The CIN may be considered the "ACO of private payers." While commercial insurance companies make up the majority of the payers for a CIN, the overall ACO concept can be applied to this model.

Providers under this model often have a guaranteed base salary with added-on incentives based on productivity (RVUs, particularly wRVUs) and non-productivity (anything that creates value for the patient). Therefore, some portion of their compensation becomes at-risk such that their maximum earning potential is contingent on the achievement of preset quality and cost metrics. Nonetheless, a fee-for-service component is retained.

Medical Home Models (PCMH and AMH)

Based in an ambulatory care setting, the medical home model may be part of an ACO/CIN system. Essentially, this model is like an ACO, except it is focused mostly on primary care with a PCP in the driver's seat. Nonetheless, varying levels of care are being consolidated and coordinated (like the CIN/ACO) and reimbursement can occur in the same ways. Payments to a medical home are dependent on the contractual agreements between the system and its payers, which may be public and private. In fact, several private payers, such as Blue Cross Blue Shield and Aetna, have implemented medical home pilots offering enhanced reimbursement for the development of such models.

Bundled Payments

Bundled payments have been around for over two decades; however, their prominence has increased exponentially in recent years. To date, mostly hospitals have been utilizing this form of payment for specific chronic diseases. Also called "episodes of care," this payment system reimburses providers by way of a lump sum that covers all healthcare services related to a specific diagnosis or procedure (or episode of care). Under this framework, providers are at-risk in that providing more care than necessary will entail loss in revenue. Thus, the bundled payment model restructures financial incentives, but also requires that providers meet certain quality targets. In addition to FFS and FFV, bundled payments may be the chief and/or only payment scheme for providers functioning within an accountable care era structure.

Demographically, the country is aging. As the baby boomers continue to age to retirement and coverage undergoes a massive expansion, the flood of older and newly insured people and their requirements for more healthcare will place even more stress on the delivery and reimbursement system.

Thus, no matter one's philosophical or even political frame of mind, we all must agree that the healthcare delivery system in the United States, and accordingly the associated reimbursement and payment structure to support this delivery system, will need dramatic overhaul in the coming years. This will affect the utilization and standards of reimbursement and the methodologies that support them to include the entire RBRVS and RVU systems.

CHALLENGES WITH THE CURRENT PAYMENT SYSTEM

The Medicare system has a long history and is the single largest purchaser of health care in the country. As such, it forms the standard for health plan payment policies in the commercial and private sectors. As discussed earlier, Medicare established the RBRVS physician fee schedule (PFS) structure in the early 1990s, introducing it in 1992. With that system, the whole concept of relative work, practice expense, and practice liability insurance—the three components of RVUs—was created. This combined relative value for each service as adjusted for geographical differences, specifically denoted as the geographic practice cost indices (GPCI), uses a multiple or standard conversion factor that is updated yearly by CMS. That payment factor became the reimbursement structure for Medicare, and, as discussed earlier, it is still in effect today.

While certainly an imperfect system, the RBRVS/RVU Medicare reimbursement system has been functional, has withstood the test of time, and continues to be operative. Moreover, hospitals and physicians, in this context, understand its structure and overall requirements. From certain standpoints, it is a predictable and functional system.

On the other hand, some people view the current system as dysfunctional. Earlier in this chapter we discussed the process of updating RVU values through the RUC. This process provides a concerted effort to update and adjust RVU values regularly—every five years. In addition, we are likely going to experience the introduction of fee-for-value payments within the concepts of care coordination programs. Nonetheless, many believe that the Medicare reimbursement system in its present state is flawed. They cite the following limitations and problem issues:

- *Evaluation and management (E&M) services value.* Many believe that the E&M codes are undervalued in terms of the overall reimbursements structure, and especially in comparison to procedural codes' values. This was somewhat supported when the RUC made rather significant upward adjustments to the E&M codes in 2007.

- ***Relative value methodologies.*** Some argue that the methodologies for assigning relative values are flawed, especially for the work component, and to some extent the practice expense components. They cite that the flaws occur in relatively new procedures, often those that are highly technology-oriented. For example, the RVU value for reading and interpreting a cardiac nuclear scan is high—much higher than some comparable codes for evaluating a cardiac patient. As care coordination codes become existent, the result likely will be further scrutiny.

- ***Undervaluing primary care physicians.*** This has been an age-old argument that appears to continue to wage throughout the industry; that is, if primary care physicians are the first (and often most influential) portal for the patient's evaluation and diagnosis, why are they not recognized through higher reimbursement and ultimately compensation? Moreover, as primary care physicians are recognized for their role in furthering wellness and overall preventative care programs, these likewise are not recognized commensurate from a reimbursement structure. The accountable care era's emphasis upon primary care physicians will further their importance within PCMHs, AMHs, ACOs, and CINs.

- ***A flawed SGR formula.*** Some would say that projecting annual cuts in physician fees of approximately 27% via the SGR (the enforcement of which has been delayed until at least January 1, 2014) has a disproportionately negative impact on primary care physicians. Again, they argue that primary care physicians are the major component in the delivery of care and should not be penalized as such.

- ***Volume incentives.*** The Medicare reimbursement system still provides incentives for increased volume, coding at higher levels, and completing more procedures/encounters. In this regard, the primary disagreement lies in the fact that reimbursement incentives are designed to reward volume, not quality or efficiency in cost containment. As the accountable care era ingredients become prominent, the importance of these volume-only incentives will decrease.

As the current Medicare system is continually evaluated, it will undoubtedly have an effect on the RVU system. For example, even if the system continues somewhat intact, as more emphasis is placed on quality and cost controls, the weighting of code values could easily change and, consequently, have a significant effect on RVU values. In turn, these RVU value changes will have a significant effect on their utilization within the practice in such areas as measuring productivity in comparison of one provider to another; ultimately they will be used as a means for calculating compensation. We have discussed all these areas throughout this book.

POSSIBLE NEW PHYSICIAN PAYMENT DELIVERY MODEL

So with these things in mind, where might the present reimbursement system be headed? Let's examine some possibilities and also consider how these relate to the RVU system.

Structure under the Advanced Medical Home

The concept of a medical home in healthcare delivery goes back several decades. A patient-centered medical home model incorporates the key elements of what has been called the advanced medical home and the personal medical home. Essentially, these mean the same thing. Specific definitions of the various pertinent terms are provided in Figure 10-1.

The basic elements of the advanced medical home model include the following: The practice or "medical home" is independently selected by the patient and as such includes a personal physician (normally a primary care practitioner). That individual has a perspective of treating the patient as a whole and leads a team of practitioners who work together for the patient's ongoing care. The lead personal physician takes responsibility for providing all of the patient's healthcare needs in all stages of life: acute care, chronic care, preventative services, and end-of-life care. If the personal physician is not qualified to provide certain levels of care, he or she is still responsible for arranging appropriate care with other professionals. The deliverables of such a system include:

- Better access to care through managed scheduling and communications;
- Improved coordination and integration of care across the continuum of providers and healthcare facilities; and
- Enhanced quality through managed evidence-based applications and therefore better decision making.

The personal physician who oversees the care of the individual is his or her constituent and supporter in facilitating treatment that is centered on high-quality coordinated medical treatment. It should be emphasized that the personal physician within the advanced medical home concept is not a "gatekeeper" who directs access to other specialists. Conversely, while advice and suggestions might be offered, the model has no punitive features if the patient chooses not to follow such advice.

As for the possible reimbursement or payment system, a bundled payment process for the personal physicians has been suggested. The bundled practice component prospectively would cover practice expenses tied to the delivery of services not covered under the current RBRVS payment system. This would include costs associated with enhanced access and communication functions, clinical integration and disease registry functions, patient medical data and referral tracking applications, evidence-based care, health information technology applications (such as e-prescribing), clinical decision support, the electronic medical record, and performance and improvement function reporting. It has been suggested that this would be based on a formula tied to the number of advanced medical home

FIGURE 10-1   Joint Principles of the Patient-Centered Medical Home

American Academy of Family Physicians
American College of Physicians
Joint Principles of the Patient-Centered Medical Home

Introduction

The American Academy of Family Physicians (AAFP) and the American College of Physicians (ACP) have developed proposals for improving care of patients through a patient-centered practice model called the "medical home" (AAFP, 2004) or "advanced medical home" (ACP, 2006). Similarly the American Academy of Pediatrics has proposed a medical home for children and adolescents with special needs.

AAFP and ACP offer these joint principles that describe the elements of the patient-centered, physician-guided medical home.

Principles

Personal physician - each patient has an ongoing relationship with a personal physician trained to provide first contact, continuous, and comprehensive care.

Physician-directed medical practice - the personal physician leads a team of individuals at the practice level who collectively take responsibility for the ongoing care of patients.

Whole-person orientation - the personal physician is responsible for providing for all the patient's healthcare needs or taking responsibility for appropriately arranging care with other qualified professionals. This includes care for all stages of life, acute care, chronic care, preventive services, and end-of-life care.

Care is coordinated and/or integrated across all domains of the healthcare system (hospitals, home health agencies, nursing homes, consultants, and other components of the complex healthcare system), facilitated by registries, information technology, health information exchange, and other means to assure that patients get the indicated care when and where they need and want it.

Quality and safety are hallmarks of the medical home:

- Evidence-based medicine and clinical decision support tools guide decision-making.
- Physicians in the practice accept accountability for continuous quality improvement through voluntary engagement in performance measurement and improvement.
- Patients actively participate in decision-making and feedback is sought to ensure patients' expectations are being met.
- Information technology is utilized appropriately to support optimal patient care, performance measurement, patient education, and enhanced communication.
- Practices go through a voluntary recognition process by an appropriate nongovernmental entity to demonstrate that they have the capabilities to provide patient-centered services consistent with the medical home model.

Enhanced access to care through systems such as open scheduling, expanded hours, and new options for communication between patients, their personal physician, and office staff.

Payment appropriately recognizes the added value provided to patients who have patient-centered medical homes. The payment structure should be based on the following framework:

- It should reflect the value of physician and nonphysician staff work that falls outside of the face-to-face visit associated with patient-centered care management.
- It should pay for services associated with coordination of care both within a given practice and between consultants, ancillary providers, and community resources.
- It should support adoption and use of health information technology for quality improvement.
- It should support provision of enhanced communication access such as secure email and telephone consultation.
- It should recognize the value of physician work associated with remote monitoring of clinical data using technology.
- It should allow for separate fee-for-service payments for face-to-face visits. (Payments for care management services that fall outside of the face-to-face visit, as described above, should not result in a reduction in the payments for face-to-face visits.)
- It should recognize case mix differences in the patient population being treated within the practice.
- It should allow physicians to share in savings from reduced hospitalization associated with physician-guided management in the office setting.
- It should allow for additional payments for achieving measurable and continuous quality improvements.

patients within the practice and other metrics such as the size of the practice and the overall scope of advanced medical home patients.

In addition, the payment policy might include a bundled care coordination component that would be prospective in nature. This would recognize the value of physician plus nonphysician support staff (both clinical and administrative) who are a part of the care coordination process.

The next component of reimbursement would be a more traditional fee-for-service reimbursement tied to encounters or visits. This would be analogous to the current Medicare RBRVS system. Thus, this portion of the reimbursement would integrate the new proposed system into the current Medicare RBRVS system. This form of reimbursement would encourage continued encounters between the physician and the patient, with checks and balances for overutilization.

Finally, the last proposed component of reimbursement would be performance-based, recognizing the attainment of defined quality and efficiency objectives. These measures could have similar characteristics to those already implemented or in process, with obvious expansion and definition. Savings that could be quantified should be shared and provided as a significant incentive for physician practices to participate and become a part of the advanced medical home model.

As a result of this proposed new model, physicians who are recognized as participants would receive prospective bundled payments for care coordination services plus reimbursement of associated practice expenses that are not covered under the current RBRVS system. These may be reimbursed through a single payment to the practice or via separate structural practice payment and physician care coordination disbursements. Some variations of reimbursement could be provided based on the risk that might reflect differences in the amount of work required and resources employed (similar to the RVU system now in place). These payments would be in addition to the physician's billing for encounter-based care covered by the current Medicare RBRVS system. Reimbursement for quality and effectiveness in outcomes would also be a part of the process.

How would these added reimbursement structures be funded? This is especially pertinent considering the fact that the typical advanced medical home model provides reimbursement for work and practice expense obligations not currently reimbursed by the Medicare system. One suggestion would be to place some of the current providers at risk for the extra cost of implementing this system if it does not achieve a specific level of savings within the Medicare system. This risk factor would not be of interest to most medical practices, particularly for those that are operating under very tight margins with little flexibility to place any additional cost at risk. Those costs might not be offset through additional reimbursement. Quality improvements that many advocates of the advanced medical home model believe would result in related cost savings to the Medicare program would in turn enable the funding of the additional reimbursement.

Advocates of the advanced medical home model have encouraged the federal government to implement a large-scale Medicare pilot project utilizing the advanced medical home care model. Such a pilot would include a bundled payment structure that supports practices that qualify as advanced medical home leaders and provide reductions in or streamlining of documentation requirements. This would result in cost savings for practices that qualify under the advanced medical home model.

Presumably, the pilot program would establish the foundation to influence changes to the Medicare Part B physician payment program to provide ongoing support for the development of the advanced medical home model nationwide. Advocates of the advanced medical home model believe that the needed additional funding could be obtained entirely from the savings within a Medicare system-wide program attributable to the advanced medical home process (documented via the pilot) and through savings from proposed processes to improve the valuation of work and practice expense services under the current RBRVS system.

The advanced medical home model can have a dramatic effect on the future of the delivery of care in the United States, but this model calls for more testing and components to be proven before a mass application occurs. Nonetheless, it has many characteristics of proven successful components, such as coordination of care, enhanced utilization of information through technology, a continuum of healthcare management with the focus on a primary physician provider responsible for the patient's care, and a constant emphasis on quality outcomes and performance-based care with associated dividends (i.e., incentive-based reimbursement) provided. As this system relates to the current RBRVS and RVUs in general, these measurements of productivity and reimbursement should continue to be a major part of the future of healthcare under this a model.

ICD-10 IMPLEMENTATION

In August 2008, the federal government proposed a new model to require all physician practices and clinical laboratories to utilize a new coding set. The current and existing code set is identified as the International Statistical Classification of Diseases, 9th edition with Clinical Modifications (ICD-9-CM). On August 21, 2008, the U.S. Department of Health and Human Services (HHS) proposed new code sets to be used for reporting diagnoses and procedures on healthcare transactions. On January 16, 2009, HHS issued a final rule mandating the implementation of the new system. Under this proposal, the ICD-9-CM code sets would be replaced with the ICD-10 code sets, effective October 1, 2013. However, on August 24, 2012, CMS' final rule 0040-F delayed the implementation of ICD-10 from October 1, 2013 to October 1, 2014.

Once implemented, ICD-10-CM will become the standard for coding diagnoses on all Health Insurance Portability and Accountability Act of 1996 (HIPAA) standard transactions. This entails an expansion of the diagnosis codes by at least five times. In theory, it should facilitate greater detail and overall scope in the coding of diagnoses and allow for more expansion in the future. Also in theory, it should improve on the description of the work being completed to accommodate the expanded technological applications within healthcare. This level of expansion will have a significant effect on the future of physician practices' and clinical laboratories' work. Additionally, it will have a significant cost effect on all sizes of practices and clinical laboratories. A recent report by Nachimson Advisors, LLC, indicates that there will be six major areas of additional costs to consider, as follows:[7]

1. Staff education and training;
2. Business process analysis of health plan contracts, coverage determinations, and documentation;
3. Changes to superbills;
4. Information technology (IT) system changes;
5. Increased documentation costs; and
6. Cash flow disruption.

While the requirement for implementation of ICD-10-CM will not have a direct effect on RVUs per se, it will have a major effect on practices, with a mandate for implementation effective October 2014.

The impact that the change in code sets will have on physician practices is too vast to estimate. Comprehensive education and training on the extensive changes will be required for every area of practice and for all medical practices. Even clinicians who do not participate in insurance transactions will now be required to understand how to document an assigned ICD-10-CM code as public health reporting or exchanging information with other practices will likely require the use of this newer code set.

Applying this to the overall practice's business processes and clinical activity will also be a requirement. Merely understanding the new code set in and of itself will be a significant requirement.

The ICD-10-CM code set likewise will have an effect on contracting with providers. Contracts that include specific diagnosis code requirements rather than medical review guidelines likely will require substantial changes. With the codes requiring more specificity, payers and the health plans that they oversee/sponsor likely will impose changes to their payment schedules that will require subsequent detail.

Improved documentation will be required before submitting claims for reimbursement.

The move to ICD-10-CM will have a profound impact on IT that is used in medical practices. Practice management systems and electronic health records (EHRs), billing service vendors, clearing houses, and all IT vendors whose products require ICD-10-CM applications will be up for review. All of these technology systems will require change and adjustment. Modifications in software will be necessary relating to insurance coverage and the basic billing system. Practice management systems that generate electronic transactions (virtually all applications) for eligibility inquiries and prior authorizations will also need modifications. EHR systems will have to accommodate the ICD-10-CM code set, especially in areas where a diagnosis code must be matched to documentation. Billing service and clearing house vendors also must adjust to be able to process the ICD-10-CM codes. Typically, dramatic system changes take extensive debugging and adjustment on the part of the users–especially for those at the practice or clinical laboratory levels.

---

[7] Nachimson Advisors, LLC. *The Impact of Implementing ICD-10 on Physician Practices and Clinical Laboratories: A Report to the ICD-10 Coalition.* October 8, 2008. Accessed June 18, 2009. Available at http://www.ahima.org/icd10/documents/nachimson.pdf.

To some extent, even patient education will be required as it relates to the changes that will appear on explanation of benefits (EOB) statements. Also, the changes in insurance plans will require further explanation to patients.

Superbills and other related encounter forms will also require significant revision due to the expanded ICD-10-CM. Old forms will no longer be usable.

In addition to the ICD-10-CM code set, there will also be a change to the inpatient hospital setting diagnosis coding. This will now become ICD-10-PCS. That new procedure coding system (PCS) uses seven alpha or numeric digits while the ICD-9-CM coding system uses three or four numeric digits. The ICD-10-CM and PCS thus incorporate greater specificity and clinical information. In theory, this should result in improved ability to measure healthcare services. It should also indicate increased sensitivity when defining both groupings and reimbursement methodologies. The system is also supposed to improve ability to conduct public health surveillance with a decreased need to include supporting documentation with claims.

As for some adjustments that will need to be considered with the change to ICD-10-CM, it is thought that health plan payment amounts will change and be based more on severity of diagnosis and changes in coverage. Thus, medical practices must analyze these changes to determine how they will affect their reimbursement and ultimately the cash they collect. Additional adjustments in the overall business office and billing processes may be required to accommodate rising or falling reimbursements. This will extend to the entire practice strategy of operations: if reimbursement is lower, the adjustments of increased productivity, increased ancillaries, and other factors must be a part of the overall practice's strategy. (This is easy to say but very difficult to incorporate. Most practices these days believe they have "stretched the rubber band" as far as they can relative to productivity and ancillary services. Nonetheless, this will have to be considered going forward.) One of the biggest questions is the uncertainty of how reimbursement will change until the actual implementation process begins. Practices will have little time to react, especially if significant cash flow interruptions result.

Dealing with multiple health plans, as virtually all practices do, will demand careful consideration of transitioning requirements, especially as they relates to coding, documentation, medical review, and reimbursement modification. Unfortunately, most health plans will be thought to have their own individual schedule that practices will have to understand and respond to. Each practice must be able to communicate their intentions for ICD-10-CM transitioning to each health plan–a monumental task.

Coordinating changes, both internally and with external health plans, will require sound business planning and ultimately implementation processes, which will include the change in IT systems, as noted above. Also, it will entail changes in communications and relations with health plans (as previously noted) and other involved parties, such as outsourced billing services, clearinghouses, etc.

Practices will have to develop a coordinated plan to assure a smooth transition and not only continuity in patient care, but perhaps more importantly, in reimbursement. A transition plan should include the following:

- *Training.* All staff should be trained, but especially those who have day-to-day interaction with coding and reimbursement. This would include the physician and other providers.
- *Internal Operations.* Business processes should be adjusted, including patient flow, documentation, charging and posting payments, and for that matter, the entire revenue cycle, to meet the new ICD-10-CM requirements.
- *Communications.* Discussions with each vendor, health plan representative, device manufacturer, and other day-to-day parties who are interacting and dealing with the practice should be scheduled to ensure good processes are in place.
- *Timeline.* A realistic schedule for implementation should be established, with as few disruptions to the practice as possible.
- *Information Systems Coordination.* All information systems should be updated and fully documented to handle ICD-10-CM coding.
- *Health Plan Participation.* Each health plan's participation and involvement in ICD-10-CM coding should be reviewed.
- *Staff Confidence.* All staff must understand and have confidence in the changes that are pending, and in fact be positive contributors to the implementation.
- *External Relationship Maintenance.* The relationships must be maintained with external parties, such as device manufacturers, vendors, health plans, and others to ensure an effective transition.
- *Internal Modeling of Changes.* Modeling should be completed within each practice prior to the actual implementation of the new program to ensure that the changes are functional and will be effective from day one.
- *External Modeling of Changes.* Testing with all outside parties should also be completed, as would be the case with the internal processes.
- *Implementation Plan.* Creating an implementation plan that assigns specific responsibilities, duties, and timelines should be a part of the overall planning and transitioning process. This must be in place prior to the actual start of the transitioning process.

While the transition process is unlikely to be easy or quick, the organizations that will find themselves at an advantage will be those that are proactive in their planning.

PROJECTED COST OF ICD-10 IMPLEMENTATION

The costs of implementing the program will vary due to the size of the practice and its overall existing sophistication and knowledge base of various applicable employees (from "front office to back office" to the providers). Suffice it to say, however, that between the education that will be required to change business processes, to specific changes in superbills, to the cost of changes in information technology, to the final processes of increased documentation, significant investment will be required on the part of virtually every practice. Indeed, this is a major change in documentation and coding procedures, and, as such, will be impossible to learn "on the fly."

On a national level, HHS estimates the conversion to ICD-10-CM/PCS costing $2.6 million per year at a present value discount of 3% and $2.3 million at a present value discount of 7% over 15 years.[8] At the organizational level, the cost will vary significantly. It would appear that given all the things that need to be addressed, from education to changes in processes, an average practice could spend as much as $10,000 to $15,000 per provider to make this transition. For a small practice of fewer than 10 physicians, a projected cost of ICD-10 implementation is roughly $83,290.[9] Likely, as is the case with most practices, the cost per provider will go down as the size of the practice increases. Certain minimum costs will be necessary for every practice; once those costs are realized, the cost per provider will be less. Regardless of practice size, the cost of implementing changes will be significant and must be considered long before the actual effective date.

In conclusion, the change from ICD-9 to ICD-10 will have a crucial effect on both the business and clinical functions of physician practices and clinical laboratories. Virtually every aspect of the medical practice and clinical laboratories' business will be affected: documentation, quality measurements, reimbursement and payment policies, staffing functions and training–even provider conduct relative to coding. Costs will be one-time as well as over a period of months and years, affected by the size of the practice and the overall complexities such as numbers of specialties. Providers will have a steep learning code relative to documentation and coding of diagnoses in ICD-10-CM. The cost of delays, additional training, and other matters likely will be a part of the overall expense, but to some extent hard to measure as this may occur through increased working hours and perhaps fewer patient encounters. It is hoped that the large price tag associated with this change will pale in comparison to the benefits garnered by it, particularly healthcare payers' and providers' access to better information for controlling care and costs.

These changes will affect RVUs and the overall productivity measurements within the medical practice and related healthcare entities in the future. The impacton medical practices' measurements of productivity and reimbursement will be significant for the years ahead.

CONCLUSION

As we consider RVUs and related matters, it is safe to say that RVUs and derivatives thereof are here to stay. They are useful in measuring direct productivity of medical practice providers; they are valuable in determining cost indicators such as staffing costs per RVU, total overhead per RVU, etc.

---

[8] Tekla et al. (2012). The Road to ICD-10-CM/PCS Implementation: Forecasting the Transition for Providers, Payers, and Other Healthcare Organizations. *Perspectives in Health Information Management*, 9(Winter), 1-15.

[9] MediMobile White Paper, "Equipping Physicians for ICD-10 Compliance: Addressing the Revenue Disruption Associated with the Transition to ICD-10," October 2012.

RVUs also are a valuable tool in managed care contracting. Because of their very nature and their roots of formation, they are applicable in the determination of fees in commercial insurance contract negotiations. Often the Medicare conversion rate per RVU is an excellent basis on which to measure the performance of commercial contracts within a given practice. No doubt, this will continue and expand in usefulness, especially as practices adopt more sophisticated information systems.

Few practices capture RVU productivity. Often, this is due to limitations of the practice management software or, in some instances, the practice is unaware of system capacity. In the future, data derived from more sophisticated practice management and EHR information systems will be used more extensively. These advanced information systems will utilize RVUs as a basic benchmark determinate of performance. Likewise, among the array of dashboard reports that the practice information system will provide, more emphasis will be placed on RVU reports.

As we now embark on the accountable care era, new entities such as PCMHs, AMHs, ACOs, and CINs will be created and functionalized. New reimbursement paradigms likely will feature fee-for-value based payments. How RVUs are used in such structures are not fully defined but appear to still be a viable feature for measuring performance.

Conclusions and Summary

We have discussed a variety of topics centering on relative value units (RVUs). We have attempted to bring the subject of RVUs up-to-date to respond to current trends in their utilization—not only in the traditional sense of productivity and compensation, but also as we consider the accountable care era changes. This chapter will summarize the key points of RVUs and consider a few areas that warrant genuine consideration not previously discussed in as much detail.

RVU PRODUCTIVITY CONSIDERATIONS

RVUs continue to serve as a great standard for the measurement of productivity, and even as we move to something other than a fee-for-volume reimbursement structure (more so to a fee-for-value), productivity will still be important. The fact that RVUs continue to be payer-blind, they do not discriminate among types or rates of reimbursement, will continue to help evaluate productivity and overall performance. While a leveled playing field will be a little different than that characteristic of our current fee-for-service reimbursement system, we believe RVUs still will be a significant factor in performance evaluation in that those standards will be considered in the context of placing RVU values on measurements of quality, cost control, etc.

With reimbursement so significantly varied from one locale to another, even within various practices within the same region, the need to standardize measurements of productivity clearly exists. It is impossible to manage without such standardization.

RVUs are the recognized standard, statistically verified and credible, for measuring medical practice provider productivity. Because RVUs have existed for many years, they are much more credible than any other unit of productivity—certainly more credible than actual dollars charged. Charges, whether adjusted or not, vary greatly from one practice to another, based on the overarching fee schedule established by that practice. While it could be argued that charges can be somewhat standardized in that they could be a derivative of Medicare rates (i.e., 150% of Medicare, 200% of Medicare, etc.), even the Medicare rates will vary slightly due to geographical adjustments. Moreover, in most practices, the largest percentage of payers come from the commercial sector, not Medicare, and their rates and fee schedules vary significantly, certainly from one payer to another. Thus, RVUs clearly are the preferred standard of measurement for productivity.

Still, "productivity" may well change in that the evaluation of productivity will be more than just sheer volume, but be inclusive of quality and cost-savings measures.

Productivity and RVUs, however, do have a great deal of variability based on the coding of the encounter by the individual practitioner. Accurate and appropriate coding of course is preferred, yet those who overcode will clearly have an overstatement of their productivity in RVUs (in charges, too) until and unless they are corrected or adjusted through audit. Most providers tend to undercode, which would also understate their total productivity in RVUs. While this is a flaw—not a fallacy—within the RVU system, it cannot be averted. It is simply a by-product of inappropriate coding, which is in and of itself another lapse that must be addressed and corrected in each practice.

Most studies on coding compliance reveal physicians coding trends as being inadequate and inaccurate, and this will probably continue to be the case under a more complex ICD-10 and fee-for-value reimbursement structure. Therefore, the need for continued compliance auditing of provider coding will be great—probably more than it has been in the past.

Even with the impending changes to a combination of fee-for-volume/fee-for-value, RVUs clearly win out as the measurement of performance and "productivity" under the new paradigm. For example, because they are compared to patient charges, it is likely that charges not only will be inconsistent from one practice to another, they may even be inaccurate. The inaccuracies are due to the coding problems outlined above (although RVUs would likewise be inaccurate as previously noted). But for purposes of measuring productivity and developing industry standards and benchmarks, RVUs clearly win out over charges.

We might also compare RVUs to encounters. However, as we move to assessing productivity based on cost control and overall quality measurements, encounters will become less significant. Nonetheless, they do measure provider workload and pace at which they work, especially in a primary care setting where patient encounters are still the greatest source of revenue. One could argue that an "encounter is an encounter," regardless of the value that is derived from it. This premise is about to change and always has been different from this premise in a fee-for-volume setting in that encounters carry different reimbursement values in a fee-for-service/volume system. Nonetheless, various encounters require different amounts of time, from the more complex and chronic to the less detailed acute cases. Even in an accountable care setting, we believe this will continue to be the case.

Prior to the introduction of RVUs, many practices considered encounters to be the best way to measure productivity in units, even though this could vary based on the sickness of the patient base of the practice. Overall, it is fair to say that a family practitioner who sees an average of 30 patients a day is "productive." Whether that 30-patients-a-day encounter rate converts to a "highly productive" RVU basis depends on the complexity of the patients, the charges that result, and ultimately the RVUs that are derived from those current procedural terminology (CPT) code assignments.

RVUs clearly expand the realm of consideration in terms of a management tool in that they allow for complexity of each case as well as other considerations such as staffing, workload, malpractice, and other metrics that are a part of the overall RVU assimilation. RVUs will continue to provide a viable management tool for evaluating performance, though they may in the future be based solely on the volume of encounters or total fee-for-volume standards. Assigning certain values (even creating new ICD-10 codes) for the measurement of quality and cost controls may well supplement the current accumulation of RVUs based strictly on utilization and volume.

RVUs also may be used as a measurement of productivity to indicate the overall overhead requirements that are justified within the practice. This will become even more important as we move to an accountable care structure. Later in this chapter we will look at cost considerations as they pertain to RVUs. But even from the standpoint of justifying the costs associated with the productivity in RVUs, it is good to consider total RVUs generated. Also, it is important that we start to measure costs and control them and, given the flexibility of RVUs, we believe this can also be effectuated, even within the new reimbursement paradigm.

Finally, as we consider RVUs as a measurement of productivity, it is also important to utilize them to complete budgetary analyses and projections. Utilizing RVUs that historically have been generated via a trending mechanism is also a great tool for management evaluation of provider productivity. Even though we have discussed the fact that every five years the RVS Update Committee (RUC) performs a more detailed evaluation and potentially changes RVU values, historically, RVUs have been fairly consistent in their values from year to year. With relative consistency in RVU values, it is possible and in fact quite viable for historical RVU production to be trended within reports; in turn, those trends ultimately can be converted to dollars that would be budgeted for overall productivity. However, as the methodologies relative to ICD-10 coding and moving to something other than a total volume-based reimbursement structure, these measurement tools may change somewhat. With that in mind, we believe RVUs will better accommodate the new reimbursement structure which will indeed be a hybrid between volume and quality/value standards.

RVUs also are relatively easy to convert into a visual presentation using graphs and charts to illustrate each individual provider's production in RVUs and to compare those results with those of their peers (see Figure 11-1) as well as with industry standards and benchmarks. Using a graph to trend RVUs with accuracy is a great tool to illustrate current and projected productivity.

Dashboard reports also should be among the tools that management uses to evaluate provider performance and specifically productivity. RVUs are easy to "dashboard" as they are succinct and easy to understand.

In summary, RVUs are easy to understand, feasible to gather as a production metric (all you need is a CPT code utilization report), and based on standards that have grown to be highly credible within the industry. Indeed, we believe RVUs, as a measurement of productivity, will continue to accommodate a new reimbursement paradigm that combines quality and quantity standards. Quantitatively, the raw data are important to tabulate, review, and understand. Obviously, it is also valuable to interpret that in terms of a management tool. From a qualitative

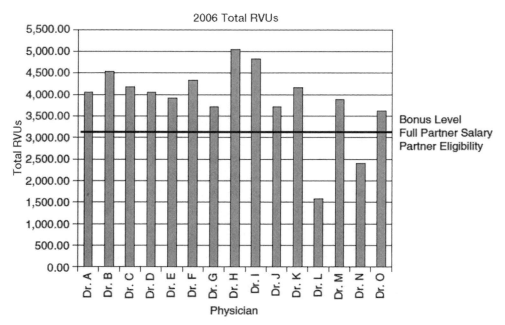

FIGURE 11-1 Total RVUs Levels per Physician in a Cardiology Practice

standard, it is also easy to utilize RVUs as a measurement of productivity to develop standards of production. However, we believe there will be opportunities to really respond to accountable care era changes, which we discussed earlier in this chapter and previously in the book.

STAFF PER RVUS

The relationship of expenses and other costs in RVUs is also a valid consideration as a part of the utilization of RVUs in management of the medical practice. For example, the largest single expense in the medical practice is personnel and benefit costs. The question of the number of staff within a practice is always a valid consideration. Is the practice staffed appropriately or is it understaffed or overstaffed, given its level of productivity? RVUs may be utilized to determine appropriate staffing, and in fact justify certain levels of staffing within the practice.

As mentioned earlier in this chapter and throughout the book, when we consider productivity in the medical practice and base it on dollars (i.e., charges or collections), it is sometimes difficult to come away with a true, valid analysis because of the huge variables within the practice due to differences in reimbursement among payers. Considering appropriate staffing as a relationship to RVUs once again tends to level the playing field in the context of the practice's staffing needs. As total RVUs (preferably work-only component RVUs [wRVUs]) are determined and are included in the dashboard and other reports of the practice, they should be compared to staffing parameters. This relates to the number of RVUs per support staff that is justified within the practice. While this may be somewhat difficult to benchmark, one way to consider it is to based it on historical productivity (i.e., RVUs). For example, if the practice has consistently produced 10,000 wRVUs per year and the support staff needed to reach this total has been 3.5, then the total wRVUs per support staff would be 2,857 (10,000/(3.5). This would provide a standard on which the practice would continue to qualify its staffing needs. For example, if the total RVUs increased to 11,428 RVUs, then perhaps an additional .5 full-time equivalent (FTE) for the provider would be justified. Of course, this may not be necessary and in fact illustrates the beauty of how RVUs can be used as a performance measurement tool. Reaching the additional number of RVUs without adding an additional .5 FTE staff results in the practice being incrementally more profitable, especially considering the fixed cost nature of staffing expense. At some point the increased RVUs may warrant additional help/staff; and utilization of such a ratio as a guide could be the best indicator of this (i.e., once the ratio reaches a certain level, additional staff are warranted).

Nonetheless, the ability to compare staff numbers on an FTE basis to total RVUs and to benchmark this over a period of years is extremely valuable.

PROVIDER PER RVUS

RVUs also can be measured on a per-provider basis. If in the above example 10,000 wRVUs becomes the expected standard per provider, then when the practice has produced 30,000 wRVUs, it should easily be able to justify three full-time providers. Further, it should have the staff and other infrastructure to support the three providers.

Measurement of productivity among providers is a dynamic situation within each practice as physicians work at a different pace and technique, which may result in significant differences in their productivity. Nonetheless, when all RVUs are added together within the practice and a standard is developed in terms of a per FTE provider number of RVUs, this can be an effective tool to use to determine not only when providers should increase in their productivity, but when additional staff providers are needed.

OVERALL COST MEASUREMENTS PER RVU

While personnel (both non-provider and provider) costs are by far the most significant expense within the practice, clearly encompassing 75% to 90% of the total overhead of the practice (again, we are including provider costs in this ratio), other costs are also important to measure in terms of RVUs. Not only can this be done with other elements of overhead even on a line-item basis, such as rent per RVU, supplies per RVU, etc., there are other metrics of measuring and defining costs per RVU.

Some of these additional metrics of measurements of costs include the following:

- Cost per encounter
- Cost per procedure
- Related comparatives

Several key indicators can be used to measure costs within an RVU analysis. Total cost per RVU should be the basis for such analyses. Moreover, these can be used for both internal management purposes and even external third-party payer contract negotiations. The total cost per RVU easily can be divided into the various RVU components, and building on such a total cost per RVU premise, the cost per procedure should be comparable to reimbursement per procedure from third-party payers, and in turn, the practice's charges on a per-procedure basis. RVUs again become a valuable tool to measure financial performance of the practice.

To rate various relationships of costs and RVUs, consider the following. These are separated by different types of RVU totals including work only, practice expense only, and malpractice:

$$\frac{\text{Provider Costs}}{\text{wRVUs}}$$

$$\frac{\text{Total Provider Compensation Expenses}}{\text{Total wRVUs}}$$

$$\frac{\text{Total Provider Benefit Expenses}}{\text{Total wRVUs}}$$

$$\frac{\text{Total Provider Compensation (Benefits and Compensation)}}{\text{Total wRVUs}}$$

Total Practice Expenses (Overhead) Per Practice Expense RVU
$$\frac{\text{Total Practice Overhead (Excluding Provider Compensation and Benefits)}}{\text{Total Practice Expense RVUs}}$$

$$\frac{\text{Total Practice Expenses Including Physician Compensation and Benefits}}{\text{Total Practice Expense RVUs}}$$

$$\frac{\text{Total Practice Expenses Including Physician Compensation and Benefits}}{\text{Total RVUs}}$$

Malpractice Expenses per Malpractice RVU
$$\frac{\text{Total Malpractice Expense}}{\text{Total Malpractice RVU}}$$

Thus, all of these provide a tangible means to consider the overhead on a per-RVU basis. In addition, cost-per-procedure calculations can be a part of the RVU analysis. A formula for this would be:

Total RVUs x Total Cost per RVU = Individual Procedure Costs

Variations of this also can be considered within the overall RVU cost analysis. Two basic ways of approaching this include lumping and splitting. Lumping RVUs entails combining together—that is, using total cost per RVU—whereas a splitting approach divides the total RVUs into individual RVU components. The nice thing about utilizing RVU data in this manner is that there is really no right or wrong methodology. Almost anything will apply that makes good business sense for the practice from a management standpoint.

COST ALLOCATIONS

Another area that is considered within the overall cost context and RVUs is allocations. Often, costs are allocated to various departments (even individual physicians) within groups. For example, a multispecialty group will allocate certain "corporate" expenses to individual specialties and/or physician practice units. In such a case, the basis and methodology for allocating can vary a great deal. Again, there is no right or wrong to this, but it does have a major impact on the overall compensation of the physicians and the financial performance of each particular department specialty, etc. In such instances, it is often best to use RVUs as a basis for allocation. While RVUs are a production metric, they can be used as a basis for allocation of overhead, especially when revenue or productivity is the best methodology. When allocating rent, RVUs may not be the best allocation approach in that rent often is allocated to various departments based on the actual space utilization. However, other expenses such as billing and revenue cycle management from a corporate standpoint is often best allocated based on some metric of revenue or productivity. And, without question, the best metric in most cases, for the reasons we have outlined throughout this book, is the RVU. Whether it's best to use total RVUs, practice expense-only RVUs, or wRVUs is somewhat debatable and is best left up to the individual analysis of the specific practice.

Thus, cost accounting can be a good application of RVUs. The methodologies for distributing expenses are a major consideration within any practice of multiple specialties, departments, ancillary services, etc. Consistency should prevail in the way costs are allocated, however. Thus, whatever methodology is chosen should be maintained for a year or more. Obviously, if the methodology is proven to be invalid even utilizing certain derivatives of RVUs, it should be adjusted. Otherwise, cost accounting is most appropriately done in medical practices utilizing RVUs as a basis for the appropriate expenses wherein measurements of productivity are the best standard for allocation.

In summary, total cost per RVU is the foundation for all RVU cost analyses. Moreover, as costs become a greater measurement tool (albeit a standard for reimbursement in the accountable care setting), such analyses will become even more important. Also, the use of RVUs in ratios of expenses as well as a methodology for allocating expenses within departments, specialties, and other units of the practice are extremely valuable tools, which likely will result in the most accurate depiction of practice performance, especially as we move to ACOs and clinically integrated organizations.

RVU COMPENSATION CONSIDERATIONS

We have reviewed RVUs' utilization in compensation plans extensively in this book; therefore, we will only touch on some highlights here . Needless to say, one of the most prominent applications of RVUs in medical practices—both hospital–owned and private—is for determining compensation. Usually these are wRVUs, but nonetheless they are excellent to use as a basis of physician compensation.

In hospital settings, wRVUs are usually applied in one of two ways. The first is to compensate the physician provider directly based on the number of RVUs that individual produces. RVUs as a derivative of the CPT code utilization are easy to translate into RVUs objectively, other than the basic subjectivity that serves as the source of the RVU derivation (i.e., the value of an RVU per a given CPT code as assigned by the Centers for Medicare & Medicaid Services [CMS]). Thus, in most compensation plans of hospital-employed physicians, the basic model utilizing wRVUs is the total RVUs times a conversion factor (sometimes called a compensation factor). However, another application of RVUs in the hospital setting is to develop production ratios of one provider to another within a given group/specialty or department.

As more and more hospitals are aligning with large groups of physicians and other providers, those alignment models also use RVUs as a basis. We believe this will continue to happen, even in the accountable care era, though the basic structures and methodologies for deriving total RVUs may be different (i.e., RVUs may be accumulated by a combination of volume/utilization and quality/cost controls). Typically, under a hospital-aligned setting, the total pool of money will be derived based on certain metrics of productivity or performance, which again can be within the context of total accumulated RVUs. It should be noted however that the accumulation of RVUs may be different in that it will not be sheer productivity only, but a combination of RVUs garnered as a result of quality and productivity. Then that pool of money is distributed within the physician group, much like they would be in a private practice. Again, this can be applied to an employment setting or a professional services agreement (PSA) setting.

To continue, if a given group's targeted production in dollars is established, that amount could be based on several derivatives such as total charges (unlikely), adjusted or net charges (probable), or an amount per RVU (a distinct possibility). That RVU can be accumulated in the future by more than just sheer productivity or accumulation of volume of services and RVUs, but more so as a hybrid, as discussed above.

Regardless, a pool of money is derived that is then distributed to the physician group in total. Within the group, the distribution of those monies could be done in several ways. One method would be assigning each individual physician/provider's ratio of his or her RVU production to the total group production. That way, RVUs have been used as an element of production and compensation, and indeed as a viable application. There are many variables or hybrids to such a model. For example, part of that pool of money could be distributed equally to mold a group-oriented mindset. The remainder could be distributed based on the ratio of productivity from one provider to another (again, possibly based on RVUs) and certainly there is the opportunity to derive a pool of money and allocate it based on other performance measurements such as quality and clinical outcomes, expense savings, etc.

Thus, in hospital applications there is a lot of opportunity to utilize RVUs in the compensation structure. That structure could be under employment and PSA. As discussed throughout this book, it is easy to "sell" physicians on RVUs and compensation because they are so logical and are the closest and most accurate thing we have in the industry to a fair standardized way of measuring productivity. Again, we think that will continue even under an accountable care era setting of reimbursement. Also, the record-keeping is relatively easy and the accuracy is really beyond question as long as the CPT code assignments are accurately compiled. Granted, under ICD-10, this will become more complex and detailed, but this same principle should still apply.

Of course, the flaw of overutilizing RVUs in a compensation model is that they are not "real money." Just because a physician produces a certain number of RVUs (i.e., wRVUs) that does not necessarily mean that a certain amount of money is available to distribute. That is why it is essential that the conversion factor or any other derivation to actual monies from RVU production is done with extensive analysis and scrutiny.

In private practices, RVUs generally are utilized as a methodology for comparing one physician or other provider's production to the total. Thus, ratios can be developed that are used to allocate pools of money for compensation. In a private group, that pool of money is usually the "bottom line." It represents the amount of monies are available to distribute to the physicians after all overhead responsibilities are addressed. For employed physicians in private groups, this may vary in that they could be utilizing an RVU model similar to that of a hospital's with a straight conversion factor formula. Again, this will require close scrutiny as to the value per RVU that is distributed to the employed physician and other providers in the practice.

Application of RVUs is also appropriate for nonphysician providers who most likely are on an incentive plan. While the formulas are similar, the metrics are usually less because the productivity and of course the compensation are almost always much less than that of a physician. Nonetheless, the same applications for nonphysician providers as physicians in compensation structures utilizing RVUs are relevant.

PLUSES AND MINUSES OF USING RVUS IN PHYSICIAN COMPENSATION

There are positives and negatives to using RVUs in physician compensation. The positives include the following:

- RVUs entail a measurement of productivity that is payer-blind and therefore standardized.
- RVUs have stood the test of time and have credibility.
- RVUs provide a consistent measurement of productivity (from year-to-year, month-to-month, etc.).
- In theory, RVUs are the most accurate measurement of the physician's time, effort, skill, and intensity involved in patient care.
- Most physicians accept RVUs as a valid measurement of productivity; moreover, they understand and appreciate the logic.
- Because of RVUs' ability to be compared to expenses, they tell a great deal more than just raw productivity does in relation to overhead and cost including that of the physician.

- RVUs can be used to measure other forms of work within an overall compensation plan, not necessarily related to patient contact. For example, RVUs can be assigned within a compensation structure for physicians' administrative time and other nondirect productivity work.
- As RVUs used in compensation formulas are prominent, the means to compare performance from one group/specialty, etc., to another has a lot of credibility.
- RVUs fit nicely into a compliance plan that requires regular coding audits to assure that productivity of the physicians is accurately documented and ultimately billed.

There also are some negatives to RVUs, especially as they are applied to physician compensation systems:

- As CMS largely establishes the RVU values and in that they are used to determine reimbursement to physicians, updates must be budget-neutral. Therefore, there are fluctuations in their values, especially as they are adjusted more so every five years by the RUC.
- Some believe that the RVU values have not kept up with the times in terms of changing medical technology, etc.
- Specialty comparisons must be carefully handled and appropriate RVU production comparisons must be derived when comparing productivity from one specialty with another.
- In a compensation structure, when RVUs are converted to compensation dollars through a conversion factor, that factor must be carefully evaluated to ensure it is economically appropriate, as RVUs do not represent "real money."
- In a private practice, measuring productivity on an RVU basis can be detrimental in that it takes the payer out of the equation, which is important in that "cash is king"
- To be most accurate, RVU calculations can become quite complex, factoring in the impact of modifiers and other factors, which many practice management systems are not able to handle.
- There is question as to the future applicability of RVUs in relation to compensation given the changes in the reimbursement environment from volume to value.
- Like most compensation systems, RVUs in compensation can be manipulated and abused.

Thus, as we consider RVUs and their application in compensation systems, we see that they are varied and have a large cross section of applicability. Many practices are now using RVUs in one form or another as a part of their overall compensation/income distribution plan formula. The fact that many are using them attests to their credibility and overall viability.

RVUS AND MANAGED CARE CONTRACTING CONSIDERATIONS

RVUs are applicable in managed care contracting. Because RVUs are a basis for Medicare reimbursement and in turn Medicare sets the standard for many private/commercial insurance negotiated rates, the connection to the resource-based relative value scale (RBRVS) system is obvious. Most commercial payers reimburse on a discounted fee-for-service basis. While some capitated contracts exist, the numbers are nominal in the United States. However, as we embark upon a fee-for-value as opposed to strict fee-for-service (i.e., discounted fee-for-service) reimbursement paradigm, the ramifications of contracting and negotiated rates are indeed changing.

When negotiating fee-for-service contracts, a specific fee schedule by CPT code usually is the result. Within a managed care contract, the practice agrees to accept that fee schedule as negotiated. Taking this one step further, many contracts offer a conversion factor multiplied by the RVU to derive reimbursement. While more complicated than a simple fee per CPT code, a basic understanding of RVUs is not that difficult to apply to such negotiations. One way of doing this is to develop a cost-based fee schedule for those evaluation and management (E&M) and other codes most often used. Essentially this comprises the practice's fee schedule based on the total cost per RVU. The multiplier comprises the profit and adjustment write-offs, resulting in the fees the practice will realize on a per-code basis. As we considered earlier, the total cost per RVU is the ratio of total practice costs to total RVUs.

Under an accountable care form of reimbursement (i.e., ACO, CIN, etc.), the form of reimbursement may be a combination of fee-for-service and fee-for-value. Under such settings, there are a lot of unknowns and as such, it remains to be seen how contracts will be negotiated. In concept, private commercial payers potentially will contract with clinically integrated organizations, and in turn those organizations will be a consortium of health systems, physicians, and other providers. Some of those physicians will be employed and some will be contracted through the CIO. The form of reimbursement likely will still entail a fair amount of fee-for-service (fee-for-volume), but clearly there will be more incentives and resultant reimbursement based on clinical outcomes and demonstrated cost savings (i.e., shared savings). Much of the talk also centers around a bundled payment wherein the CIO will receive a total payment for the full continuum of services from all providers, and in turn will then be obligated to distribute that total bundled payment to the constituent members of the CIO.

As to how managed care contracting will take place and how RVUs will fit in, there are still a number of unanswered questions. However, we assume that the RBRVS RVU system will continue to exist as will the ability to derive total RVUs from the ICD coding processes. Even with reimbursement based on something other than volume of services, we believe there are opportunities to use RVUs that would be tied to ICD codes that are not strictly based on volume and productivity, but more so a result of measurement of quality and cost savings. Again, there is much to be resolved in these areas and it will be imperative that all providers of health care work together to sort out the issue and try to make the system work under such a new reimbursement structure.

In reality, most managed care organizations (MCOs) have a level of sophistication that will accommodate any new reimbursement structures. However, at the time of this writing, few MCOs are reaching out and insisting on a new payment structure; therefore, for at least the near-term, managed care contracting will probably have little (if any) changes. At the core of the RVU structure and contract negotiations is the Medicare conversion factor as a derivative of reimbursement. Many times, MCOs offer a percentage of the practice's current fee schedule and, for example, will establish reimbursement at say, 150% of Medicare rates. The negotiation process would then proceed from there. In its basic interpretation, such a calculation would follow the formula below for non-Medicare payers:

Total RVUs x Conversion Factor = Reimbursement

A conversion factor in this case is simply that number by which the RVUs are multiplied to calculate a reimbursement for the code. It converts RVUs into dollars—the way it is utilized in many compensation systems. If the total RVUs and the actual reimbursement for each code are known, the mathematical calculation of simply dividing the reimbursement amount by the total RVUs will derive the conversion factor. This can be done across the entire practice for all CPT codes, allowing a breakdown of those codes into ranges such as the E&M codes, medicine codes, surgery codes, etc. Payers will reimburse at different rates, depending on these overall major classifications.

Utilizing a spreadsheet to summarize these totals is recommended. First, multiply the practice's fee for each procedure to derive the gross charge total. Then, multiply that total number by the managed care contract's proposed reimbursement to derive the volume-adjusted rate. Subtract the total gross charges from the managed care contract reimbursement for all codes to derive a dollar variance. Finally, divide the total managed care contract reimbursement by the total gross charges to derive the discount percentage.

Thus, RVUs are a major application within such a fee schedule. A weighted average should be used when looking at all of the various payers, depending on the volume of patient base that each payer represents within the practice.

Another methodology that MCOs use is to base their fee schedules on a percentage of Medicare. This is done by taking the current year's Medicare conversion factor and offering the medical practice a multiplier that effectively results in a new conversion factor to then multiply by RVUs. For example, let's take the 2009 Medicare conversion factor of $36.0666. If the managed care contracting organization offers a multiplier of 1.5 (150%) of Medicare, that new conversion factor would be $54.0999 (1.5 x $36.0666). To derive reimbursement, the new conversion factor is simply multiplied by the RVU value for each particular code. Usually in such a case, the managed care contracting organization will adjust for geographical practice cost indices, not unlike that of the Medicare reimbursement itself.

Some payers have moved away from Medicare as a basis for their fee schedule in that CMS makes fairly regular changes (at least yearly) to their conversion factor and other metrics. Thus, a negotiated conversion factor is utilized. This is similar to a compensation plan utilizing a conversion factor wherein it is the conduit between production (i.e., RVUs) and compensation. This methodology is applied similarly to overall reimbursement. However, when dealing with reimbursement, we are considering total RVUs, not just the wRVU or the other two components exclusively.

Another critical component of managed care contracting when the payer uses Medicare as a standard is the RBRVS year being used. This can make a significant difference in the overall reimbursement, given the somewhat dramatic changes in fee schedules from year to year within the RBRVS system.

RVUS AND CONTRACT NEGOTIATIONS

There is still tremendous opportunity for the practice to be prepared with sufficient information to use in its contract negotiation process. Although many believe the future will be a combination of fee-for-volume and fee-for-value, for the time being the fee-for-service structure is still the primary form of contract negotiations. Knowing the details of the individual codes relative to an accurate cost factor plus the amount required in reimbursement per code in order to generate a reasonable return on investment is invaluable to the practice. Even under a new reimbursement structure, this knowledge is going to be extremely important, especially if providers have to demonstrate some forms of shared savings.

For now, those contracts that are negotiated on an RVU conversion factor basis should be considered based on the cost per reimbursement code as noted above. In the same way, establishing a conversion factor in income distribution or compensation plan for physicians and other providers is important, knowing the appropriate conversion factor on total RVUs is essential to successful contract negotiations too. In addition, it is important to know the specific RVU year that the MCO is using. The correct RVU year should be used to calculate both the current and proposed fee schedules to determine the changes (up or down) proposed by the MCO. This should be analyzed by simply listing the top codes that are used within a particular practice or specialty, comparing those with the RVU values for the last two to three years, and then multiplying those by the proposed conversion factors from the proposed rate of reimbursement versus the current rate of reimbursement. This will derive total dollars. The differences can then be converted to percentages to illustrate the true change. We emphasize that this should be done on a code-by-code basis, not in total. From a practical standpoint, this would have to be done on an individual code-by-code basis with the varying RVU totals per code.

As we progress into the accountable care era, it will be important to know the basis for the MCO's reimbursement structure. If Medicare continues to be that foundation for deriving their structure, there may be relatively few changes, at least from the methodology for determining an appropriate rate (i.e., percent of Medicare, etc.). However, as the reimbursement structure changes to a bundled payment within a clinically integrated organizational setting, there may be new things to consider—new basis upon which the MCO would derive its proposed reimbursement rate.

Moreover, if we are now speaking about a reimbursement rate that encompasses the continuum of virtually all providers of care (as opposed to ambulatory versus inpatient versus other provider services being individually contracted and paid), the entire negotiation process will be dramatically different. As to how RVUs will play into this, again, there are many unanswered questions. For ambulatory providers (especially physician practices), the ability to track and evaluate RVUs (even if some of those RVUs are tied to ICD codes that are something other than productivity based) should result in a comparable approach. In other words, if total RVUs can be derived and a rate per RVU likewise derived (a conversion factor), then the ability to negotiate in a fairly quantitative straight-forward manner (such as is the case today) should continue. Complicating this however will be the creation of provider consortiums such as ACOs and clinically integrated organizations.

OTHER FORMS OF PRODUCTIVITY CONSIDERATIONS

In addition to "straight RVUs," there are other forms of productivity that have characteristics of RVUs or are derivatives thereof. While we offer a brief discussion of these items, we emphasize that RVUs' complexion may well change in the course of moving to a new reimbursement paradigm. Thus, deriving an RVU based on something other than the volume of work performed by the provider will be likely. Doing this as a function of time may also be a strategy.

Time Value Units

Time relative value units are an interesting approach to measuring productivity in such units. Basically, instead of the traditional RVU measurement based on the actual work and related cost of performing the professional services, the unit of productivity is based on the amount of time required to complete. This has a somewhat narrow application and as such is not as standardized as the RVU system. It seems to have its greatest application in specialties where the time that is required to perform a particular function is a better methodology than the RVU system. One such example is cardiology. Many cardiology practices have developed a system similar to an RVU measurement of productivity, but apply the units based on the time required to complete each professional work product. Certainly every physician's time is valuable, but we also know that in most specialties, physicians, as in any other profession, work at a different pace and rate. In a primary care practice, some physicians can easily see 30 patients a day and be effective in the process, while others are hard-pressed to see more than 20; yet they are working just as diligently. However, within the time RVU system, we assume that time is a much more relevant and appropriate way of measuring productivity than the traditional ways that are akin to encounters, RVUs, and indeed actual dollars generated.

As we consider time RVUs and apply them in the example of a cardiology practice, it is evident that certain procedures may require less time than others, yet in terms of the overall cardiology practice, the processes that take more time may be valued at fewer RVUs. For example, a cardiologist who is trained to read echocardiograms can do so within a relatively short period of time–perhaps as little as five minutes—whereas an encounter of a diagnostic nature directly with the patient will undoubtedly take much longer. Yet in looking at RVU values, the value of reading the echocardiogram is much greater than the E&M code that would support the diagnostic encounter. This could be argued from either point of view and ultimately should be the decision of the physicians and administrative leadership of the practice as to which standard is most appropriate. In some practices, the utilization of both time RVUs and RVUs is applied with a weighting of the two. For example, perhaps 50% of the productivity is weighted on the basis of RVUs with the remaining 50% weighted to the time RVUs.

Keep in mind that this is not a standardized system—it must be developed within each individual practice. The flaws of the time RVU system are obvious: since there is no standardization, the individual practice must discern the values of the various codes and the time that is required to complete them versus other codes that are used within the practice. Similarly, there is no benchmark data to compare these values, and thus, utilization of time RVUs is strictly an internally derived process.

The pace of physicians still has applicability in a time RVU system. For example, even though a cardiologist who reads an echocardiogram might be awarded a certain time RVU, the amount of time that one practitioner requires to complete this process versus another could differ significantly. Yet within the time RVU system, the rates of productivity would be assigned in a standardized manner, regardless of the amount of actual time required. (However, the amount of time RVUs awarded would be based on long-standing history and supporting analysis to derive a reasonable amount of time for completing such procedures.)

Another somewhat negative point is that there is no direct correlation between the actual time spent and the reimbursement received from third-party payers. This could also be asserted with RVUs, though the standardization of RVUs that has been developed over the years does attempt to address this matter, at least to some extent, whereas time RVUs have no direct correlation.

Time RVUs are an interesting approach to measuring productivity and have some applicability, though quite narrow. The vast majority of practices should apply the RVU system prior to any consideration of a time RVU system.

A caveat to the time RVU system could be that certain codes or procedures might be assigned a time RVU value instead of an RVU value. In other words, if the practice internally decides that it is appropriate to assign a greater value to certain procedures or encounters, the practice might use a time RVU instead of a wRVU for measurement of that level of productivity. Once again, this would have to be applied consistently and only utilized after thorough research. All parties within the practice would have to agree that this is applicable.

A word of caution is warranted: any time a practice moves away from the standardization that is inherent to utilizing an RVU-based system, it is jeopardizing the integrity of their overall productivity measurement process. Nonetheless, time RVUs may have some application in certain practices—either in whole or in part.

Awarding RVUs for Non-Procedural Work

RVUs have been used as a unit of productivity measurement for non-procedural work. In the course of our discussion related to accountable care, we have suggested that CPT codes may be created to measure performance relative to cost savings and even quality outcomes. In other words, if a certain level of cost savings is achieved, a particular code may be awarded to be billed and then a corresponding RVU associated with that code. In that manner, RVUs would continue to be a measure of "productivity."

Currently there are alternative forms of measuring productivity via awarding work that has been completed but not directly tied to a CPT code and a standardized RVU. There are many other important performance measurement tools that are qualitative as opposed to quantitative. The question always arises during such discussions as to how physicians are recognized for their performance in areas of qualitative matters. Needless to say, this also has much application when developing and administering an income distribution plan for physicians. Many believe that their compensation, while largely based on quantitative productivity performance, should not be 100% based on that. There are many other areas of qualitative performance that are almost as important, if not equal in importance. One might also argue that without these qualitative standards, the quantitative performance is not as valid and over time will actually suffer.

As a result, many practices, hospitals and other employers of physicians, and other healthcare providers will carve out at least a portion of their productivity measurement process (and indeed in many cases, their compensation plan) that is otherwise based on RVUs by awarding additional RVUs or measurements of productivity for qualitative performance. Needless to say, this becomes a subjective process. It is actually more subjective in many cases than the time RVU process discussed above. Examples of qualitative performance could include:

- Service to the community
- Administrative duties
- Administrative adherence and "good citizenship"
- Clinical outcomes and quality measurements
- Academic responsibilities including supervising residents
- Research
- Patient satisfaction

In compensation plans we often call these things "soft" incentives. While they are not based on "hard" quantitative performance that is ultimately tied to reimbursement, they nonetheless are important in the overall process.

In application, these soft incentives are reviewed and an RVU (again, usually wRVU) value is assigned to them. For example, let's say a physician is asked to participate in formulating certain clinical protocols within a specific specialty service line on behalf of the hospital. In this example, the physician is employed by the hospital. Completing this assignment will require the physician's time and energy. While the assignment may be performed after normal work hours, it nonetheless is a part of the overall professional time that the physician spends within the employment of the hospital. As such, the hospital may assign (credit the physician with) a certain number of wRVUs relative to the responsibilities of performing the assignment.

In a compensation plan application, those RVUs would be accumulated along with the other RVUs tied directly to encounters and/or procedural work and the physician thus compensated for both the "soft" work and the more quantitative professional fee generation (through wRVU productivity credit).

A word of caution is required here. While awarding wRVUs for soft work (i.e., more qualitative performance) is sometimes justified, it can get out of hand quickly. Even though there are not direct charges resulting from such work, in the long run, there may be improvements in productivity and revenue due to the work that is done in such qualitative areas.

Another example would be a physician who is assigned to work within the community, perhaps giving lectures or even being a part of a community health fair event. While this work does not directly result in revenue, it should, on an overall basis, provide a result. Plus, it provides more education for wellness and other important services to the community. Awarding wRVUs for such work is appropriate; however, it must be done with some sense of fiscal propriety.

When awarding wRVUs in this manner, we recommend that each individual situation be reviewed on its own merits. Analytically, this can be based on the amount of time that is spent by the physician, similar to time RVUs. For example, hypothetically if a family practitioner is reasonably able to generate five wRVUs in an average hour of patient encounter time, perhaps that would be the number that is awarded for community service and other related qualitative services. Even in this case we would recommend that it be discounted at least by 50% as clearly the value of such work does not carry the overall fiscal significance as does actual patient encounter production. It is important that ceilings be established on such soft incentives and wRVUs awarded. For instance, perhaps the employer should establish a maximum number of hours that would be awarded for each physician over a specified period of time. This would also need to be considered in the overall analysis and pro forma that is completed in order to decide the value in wRVUs of such functions.

Awarding RVUs for nonproductivity (patient encounter) work can also occur in other areas. For example, the case is made often that in a compensation plan that is tied to wRVU production only (and often compensation derived from a simple conversion factor formula), there are no incentives for expense control. In such instances, again with completion of analysis and due diligence, the employer can award additional wRVUs if the physician achieves expense control in areas over which he or she has direct oversight. In turn, those wRVUs become just like any other productivity-based wRVU and are converted into compensation via the conversion factor process. Thus, we have taken an essentially productivity-only based compensation plan and converted it into a more cross-sectional plan that considers rewarding the physician for other important areas such as expense control. Likewise, this can be said for the soft incentives as a part of the overall compensation plan.

Even if the practice is not on a compensation plan tied to wRVUs, it may be appropriate to award wRVUs to the physicians for measurements of their overall productivity in comparison to their peers for such soft incentives. In a private practice this could apply not only to things like expense control, but to administrative duties and responsibilities. For example, a physician who is serving as the president of a multi-specialty group obviously spends a great deal of additional time in administrative and management oversight. That person may be awarded an agreed-upon number of wRVUs that would be added to his or her total production-based wRVUs. In turn, that total number of wRVUs would be used to compare with other associates in the practice total productivity. Again, to a large extent, that total may be used in designating certain compensation, or in a private group, the total would be considered in relation to the total RVUs of the practice and used as a ratio for allocation of bonuses, etc.

Thus, the standards that are applied to the entire RVU system have great application for areas of productivity assignment and measurement that are sometimes difficult to quantify within a traditional practice data-gathering sense. In other words, because no direct productivity dollars are generated for this work, it is difficult to arbitrarily assign "dollars" to these functions and add them to the actual productivity dollars that a physician produces. Alternatively, using RVUs in this process brings a great deal more credibility and justification. But again, we emphasize that RVUs are not "real money" and are at best subjective in this type of application. Thus, it is essential that conservatism and due diligence prevail in assigning wRVUs in this manner. In fact, in most cases we would recommend that an independent party (nonpractice employee or physician) complete such analysis and assist the practice or hospital in deriving the wRVUs that would be awarded for such functions.

Encounters

We would be remiss if we did not consider measuring productivity in simple encounters. While encounters are still somewhat meaningful and therefore could be used for the overall analysis of performance and productivity, their meaning will decrease within our accountable care changing world. An encounter between a patient and physician in certain settings still has merit for measurement of productivity. RVUs take into consideration the time and intensity of the encounter whereas the actual encounter is simply based on the number that the physician realizes (in visits). Encounters were a useful measurement of productivity prior to the introduction of RVUs. For certain specialties, they are probably the best means of tracking provider productivity other than actual dollars. However, with the introduction and the maturation of the RBRVS and RVU system, there is no question that RVUs are a much more reliable and accurate means of deriving nondollar productivity.

Having said this, encounters still have some validity within practices, especially nonprocedurally oriented specialties. Primary care practices still provide a great deal of emphasis and indeed insights relative to productivity and encounters. For example, the pediatrician in the busy season who sees 40 patients a day is considered to be quite productive, whereas the pediatrician who may only see 25 patients per day is considered average or below. Thus, encounters have some validity in the process. But at the same time, the way RVUs are utilized and assimilated, they tell the practice so much more about performance and overall standards. Once again, measuring RVUs in comparison to others within the practice and industry benchmarks is much more reliable than simple encounters.

Thus, encounters can be used and still considered within certain settings, especially absent a fully developed and implemented accountable care reimbursement structure. Even then, measuring performance through encounters may still be an appropriate tool of management evaluation. Interestingly enough, as the reimbursement structure moves away from volume and toward number of encounters as a basis of success, we may measure encounters in the context of how few they should be as opposed to how many.

CONCLUSION

In this chapter we have considered various components within the utilization and application of RVUs, all in the context of an impending (and likely) changing reimbursement paradigm. Still, RVUs win out as the most useful form of performance measurement outside of the actual income statement itself. If the utilization of RVUs in an accountable care setting can be structured such that RVUs are still a key component of the accumulation of overall performance in both volume and value terms, they survive and continue to be the most useful form of management evaluation.

Index

GreenbranchPublishing
www.greenbranch.com (800) 933-3711

TheJournalofMedicalPracticeManagement©

Fast Practice: Medical Practice Information at the Speed of SoundNewsletterandAudio

Books and eBooks

Neil Baum/Catherine Maley/Andrew Schneider: Social Media for the Health Care Profession

Randy Bauman: Time to Sell? Guide to Selling a Physician Practice: Value, Options, Alternatives, 2nd Edition

Joel Blau/Ron Paprocki: The Prescription for Financial Health:Physician's Guide to Financial Planning

Judy Capko: Secrets of The Best-Run Practices, 2nd Edition

Judy Capko: Take Back Time: Bringing Time Management to Medicine

Judy Capko/Cheryl Bisera: The Patient-Centered Payoff: Driving Practice Growth Through Image, Culture, and Patient Experience

Frank Cohen/Owen Dahl: Lean Six Sigma for the Medical Practice

Owen Dahl: Think Business! Medical Practice Quality, Efficiency, Profits

Owen Dahl: Guide to Medical Practice Disaster Planning

Jeffrey Gorke: The Physician's Guide to the Business of Medicine: Dreams & Realities

John Guiliana/Hal Ornstein: 31½ Essentials for Running Your Medical Practice

Marc Halley/Halley Consulting Group: The Medical Practice Start-Up Guide

Wendy Lipton-Dibner: MAD Leadership for Healthcare: Proven Strategies to Get People to Do What You Want Them to Do

Betsy Nicoletti: Auditing Physician Services and E/M Coding

Betsy Nicoletti: The Field Guide to Physician Coding, 2nd Edition

Luis Pareras: Innovation & Entrepreneurship in the Healthcare Sector: Idea to Funding to Launch

Kevin Pho/Susan Gay: Establishing, Managing, and Protecting Your Online Reputation: A Social Media Guide for Physicians and Medical Practices

Richard Reece: The Health Reform Maze: A Blueprint for Physician Practices

Max Reiboldt/Coker Group: RVUs at Work: Relative Value Units in the Medical Practice, 2nd Edition

Laura Sachs Hills: How to Recruit, Motivate & Manage a Winning Staff

Don Self/Steve Verno: ERISA: The Medical Practice Guide to the Employee Retirement Income Security Act

Lawrence Shapiro: Quality Care, Affordable Care: How Physicians Can Reduce Variation and Decrease the Cost of Health Care

Ron Sterling: Keys to EMR/EHR Success, 2nd Edition   Winner! HIMSS Book of the Year Award

Drew Stevens: Patient Acceleration: Helping Chiropractors Maximize Patient Volume and Revenue

Alan Whiteman: Cutting Costs in the Medical Practice, 2nd Edition